*Renaissance
of Wonder*

Renaissance of Wonder

The Fantasy Worlds of C. S. Lewis, J. R. R. Tolkien, George MacDonald, E. Nesbit and Others

Marion Lochhead

HARPER & ROW, PUBLISHERS

SAN FRANCISCO

Cambridge
Hagerstown
Philadelphia
New York

London
Mexico City
São Paulo
Sydney

1817

FIRST U.S. EDITION

Library of Congress Cataloging in Publication Data

Lochhead, Marion.
   Renaissance of Wonder.

   Reprint of the ed. published by Canongate, Edinburgh, under title: The renaissance of wonder in children's literature.
   Includes bibliographical references and index.
   1. Children's literature, English—History and criticism.
2. Fantastic literature, English—History and criticism. I. Title.
PN1009.Z6L6   1980   820'.99282   80–7753
ISBN 0–06–250520–3

---

80 81 82 83 84 10 9 8 7 6 5 4 3 2 1

ACKNOWLEDGMENTS

The author wishes to thank the following for the use of quotations from copyright works: George Allen & Unwin Ltd for quotations from J. R. R. Tolkien's *Tree and Leaf, The Hobbit* and *Lord of the Rings* and Joy Chant's *Red Moon and Black Mountain;* The Bodley Head Ltd for quotations from *Perelandra* by C. S. Lewis; Dr Katharine Briggs for extracts from two of her books, *Hobberdy Dick* and *Kate Crackernuts;* Burke Publishing Co. Ltd for small passages from *Brogeen Follows the Magic Tune* and *Guests at the Beech Tree* by Patricia Lynch; Chatto & Windus Ltd for quotations from *The Two Fiddlers* by George Mackay Brown and *Over Sea, Under Stone, The Dark is Rising* and *Greenwitch* by Susan Cooper; William Collins Sons & Co. Ltd for quotations from *Crossings* by Walter de la Mare, *Surprised by Joy* and the Narnian tales by C. S. Lewis, and *The Weirdstone of Brisingamen, The Moon of Gomrath, The Owl Service* and *Elidor* by Alan Garner; J. M. Dent & Sons Ltd for extracts from Patricia Lynch's books, *A Storyteller's Childhood* and *The Turf-Cutter's Donkey;* Gerald Duckworth & Co Ltd for brief quotations from Walter de la Mare's *Three Mulla Mulgars;* Faber & Faber Ltd for quotations from *With Angus in the Forest* by Meta Mayne Reid, *The Children of Green Knowe* by Lucy Boston and *Thursday* by Catherine Storr; Victor Gollancz Ltd for short extracts from *Wizard of Earthsea* and *The Farthest Shore* by Ursula Le Guin; Hamish Hamilton Children's Books Ltd for quotations from William Mayne's *Earthfasts;* George G. Harrap & Co. Ltd for quotations from *Beadbonny Ash* by Winifred Finlay; A. M. Heath & Co. Ltd, Authors' Agents, for quotations from Joan Aiken's *Winterthing;* William Heinemann Ltd for short extracts from *The Driftway* by Penelope Lively; Macmillan Ltd for quotations from *The Land of Youth* by James Stephens and Walter de la Mare's introduction to James Stephens' *The Crock of Gold;* Penguin Books Ltd for a quotation from *Gods and Myths of Northern Europe* by Hilda Ellis Davidson; A. D. Peters & Co. Ltd for extracts from Ray Bradbury's *Hallowe'en Tree* and The Society of Authors for quotations from John Masefield's *Box of Delights* and works by Walter de la Mare, and it is hoped that any other copyright holders whom it has not been possible to trace will accept an equally grateful expression of appreciation.

Thanks are also due, and are most gladly paid to Trevor Royle for his kind Preface; to Paul Harris for help and encouragement during the revision of the book; and to Jean Desebrock for most careful and helpful editing. Finally I would like to thank Angus and Stephanie Wolfe Murray for their invaluable help just before this book went to press.

PREFACE

"I am almost inclined to set it up as a canon that a children's story that is enjoyed only by children is a bad children's story. The good ones last."

What C. S. Lewis said about fairy stories has been diligently applied by Marion Lochhead to this book. There is no-one more suited than Miss Lochhead to write about the development of the world of fantasy and faery from its nineteenth-century renaissance to the great masters of the genre, C. S. Lewis and J. R. R. Tolkien. Miss Lochhead is well versed in the Victorian domestic scene and there is little about Victorian childhood that has escaped her scrutiny. Her two earlier books *Their First Ten Years* and *Young Victorians* (both John Murray) have become minor classics and she herself has written magically for children in *On Tintock Tap* (The Moray Press).

In a century plagued by the doubt created by scientific discovery and rational thought, and at a time when the whole basis of Christian civilisation was being questioned, the Victorian mind was ripe for capture by the alternative world of faery. As man developed a hard and artificial industrialism, worked for profit and made slaves of his fellows, writers like George MacDonald and Mrs Molesworth helped their readers to escape from social and political reality into a world where the lordly power of faery still held sway. In particular, Miss Lochhead has related George MacDonald's awareness of an inner world and of time beyond our own to his Celtic heritage.

Neither MacDonald nor any other writer invented the faery world: they looked again at a world which was rapidly disappearing and which was largely based on folk-lore and folk-myth. It was the world of King Orfeo, Tam Lin, and Thomas the Rhymer amongst many others. Most of the stories in that tradition were not originally told for children, but, as they were passed on from generation to generation, only the good ones survived. In turn they were overheard by children and became adopted by them because children enjoyed listening to them. The stories of Curdie, the Princess and the Goblin, Griselda, Narnia and Middle Earth are equally good to read, and, as Miss

Lochhead makes very clear, they stand an equally good chance of survival.

Both George MacDonald and C. S. Lewis rightly acknowledged their debt to the Scottish folk heritage. Not the least of the pleasures in the appearance of this book is that not only is Miss Lochhead a Scot, but her book appears in the lists of an Edinburgh publisher.

TREVOR ROYLE

Dedicated to
AGNES ETHEL MACKAY
and
MARION MELVILLE
for long friendship, and
happy memories of France

"Les mythes nés de l'antiquité foisonnent, innombrables, et ne sont pas près de mourir; aujourd'hui encore notre imagination en est nourrie."
— Marion Melville in *Les Châteaux Imaginaires.*

CONTENTS

Chapter 1

THE MYTH-MAKER

George MacDonald and *Phantastes*

The nineteenth century saw a renaissance of wonder in books for children, as well as in poetry and religion. What the Oxford Movement did for the Church by reviving her sense of worship and mystery, what the Romantic poets and, in their own fashion, the Pre-Raphaelites did for literature and art, was done for the young by tales of enchantment. The magic casements had long been closed—but shuttered, perhaps, rather than closely barred, and the shutters always a little open to the light. In the Age of Reason, books for children had been reasonable, instructive and edifying, although not without interest of plot—as in the tales of Maria Edgeworth, and even in Mrs Sherwood's *The Fairchild Family*. These rational and moral writers deplored fairy-tales as folly, and the godly frowned upon them as lying fables.

From time to time the shutters swung back: the magic casements were opened. Old tales were told again by mother or grandmother or nurse. Then appeared *Granny's Wonderful Chair*[1] by the blind story-teller Frances Browne, an Irishwoman with an hereditary gift. The idea is delightful: that a child can sit in a chair and say, "Chair of my grandmother, tell me a story," or, "Chair of my grandmother, take me on a journey." The setting is homely. The child Snowflower lives with her grandmother, Dame Frostyface, in a poor cottage. Dame Frostyface must visit an ancient aunt in the North Country and must leave Snowflower behind, for, as she tells her, "My aunt is the crossest woman alive and never liked young people." The chair is Snowflower's companion and guardian. At the child's bidding it will tell a story, and take her upon a journey, which, like all the journeys in good fairy-tales, ends in a palace—where Dame Frostyface is brought to join her granddaughter and is installed with a fine new spinning-wheel of ivory.

This book may be seen as a prelude or dawn-song. The

[1] See Bibliography

1

renaissance proper began with a Scot, George MacDonald. He was born in Aberdeenshire and brought up in the country town of Huntly. His father was a miller. All the Scottish and Celtic heritage of magic and tales of enchantment lay behind him. His own mind was that of a poet and seer. He was a true maker, and he made new myths. To call him a Scottish Hans Andersen would be making too large a claim, for his genius was sometimes flawed and diluted, and he wrote too copiously outside the range of myth and fairy-tale. But these two men shared the gift of turning homeliness into beauty and strangeness, and of giving awareness to flowers and trees, as well as to people and animals. Hans Andersen was coming into the English nursery at this time through the translation of his tales by Mary Hewitt. But George MacDonald's supreme and unique gift was his ability to blend holiness with magic. Morality had long been present, indeed over-emphasised, in childrens' literature. It was thrust upon the young. However, the essence of goodness, which is true holiness, and the joy which is part of sanctity, had been unknown.

MacDonald's first book was the long poem *Within and Without*. The title is a key phrase for MacDonald: he created a world in which it is easy to pass from without to the hidden reality within. Then in 1858 came *Phantastes*,[2] which he described as "a Faerie Romance", though one for men and women rather than for children. Yet for children, too, there is allurement here. The story opens most engagingly. The hero, Anados, discovers a secret compartment, like a tiny room, in an old desk, and from it steps a little woman who grows tall and beautiful. She is the first of MacDonald's queen-goddess-mother figures. "You shall find your way into fairyland tomorrow," she promises, and next morning Anados finds his room transformed. It is a room such as many of MacDonald's original readers would have known, including any children who looked into the book. Their nurseries would not have been like this, but their parents' bedrooms and the spare bedrooms might well have been furnished like that of Anados, with heavy carved furniture, green carpet, flower-patterned curtains and marble wash-stand. When Anados wakens, he finds himself in a woodland glade. The green carpet has become grass under his feet; the curtains have turned to living flowers, the carvings to branches and foliage. From what was the wash-stand falls a stream of water which he follows into the magic forest and into fairyland. He comes to a cottage "built of the stems of small trees set closely together", with four great trees forming the corners, their branches arching and intertwining above the roof. Inside it is furnished "with rough chairs and tables from which even the rough bark had not been removed." It is an enchanted cottage, better even than a castle or a palace, and the woman who lives there is kind, welcoming the traveller with food—and a warning. The story thereafter develops beyond the scope of childish imagination. More will be said of it later. There is something in it of the Divine Comedy. Like Dante, the hero finds himself in a dark wood, and, although he does not descend into Hell, there are glimpses of hellish evil. His could be described as a journey through Purgatory. All MacDonald's fantasies are full of hints and glimpses of Catholic teaching.

In 1867 MacDonald published a book specifically for children entitled *Dealings with the Fairies*. This is a collection of fairy-tales full of traditional magic but with a new ingredient: MacDonald's own genius. The stories include *The Shadows*, *The Carasoyn* and *The Golden Key*—the last also a significant title, for the key is an important symbol. The children in this story must find the key which will open the door to the hidden place, the kingdom within, but it is only after years of wandering and separation, when they are both old, that they find it and open the door. MacDonald, having found his own golden key, gave it away to any who cared to have it and to follow him into his inner kingdom of magic and holiness.

In 1870 came *At the Back of the North Wind*[3], which for many readers is the best-loved of all MacDonald's books. It was followed in 1872 by *The Princess and the Goblin*[4] and, much later, by its sequel, *The Princess and Curdie*[5]. In 1895 he published another fantasay, an allegory or dream-sequence entitled *Lilith*[2]. In the intervening years he had written many novels of varying quality, rarely without a gleam of poetry, holiness and delight. The fire of his genius was like the peat-fire of the Highlands—never extinguished, but smoored* at nightfall with invocation and blessing, and stirred at dawn, again with invocation, to brightness and warmth.

MacDonald was a Highlander and a Celt by heredity and tradition although he was born in the north-east and not in Gaeldom. In the Celtic mythology which he inherited, the way

* Covered

into faery is a very short step from this world and the journey may be very swift. And a man may stay in faery for what appears to be only a day and a night, only to find he has been absent from this world twenty, fifty or a hundred years; or he may stay there for what seems like years and find he has been absent only an hour. Anados in *Phantastes* goes into the enchanted wood two days after his twenty-first birthday. On his return he is received by his sisters "with unspeakable joy" for he has been absent twenty-one days, which must have seemed like twenty-one years. The children in *The Golden Key*[6] go on a lifelong journey starting from the wood which is the entrance to faery, and they never come back. The end of their journey is in Paradise.

MacDonald drew, consciously or unconsciously, from his Celtic heritage. He used it and added to it. He followed set patterns but wove his own web of beauty, terror and wonder. He brought back the element of evil and showed the primeval antagonism between darkness and light, the conflict which began in lost Eden. In recompense he brought back also innocence, holiness and divinity. There is an element in his tales which is utterly beyond the familiar nursery naughtiness and morality.

Tame morality is absent from his stories; so is mere whimsy. There is nothing at all of what C. S. Lewis, his disciple, later denounced as "the increasing prettification and triviality" of some late Victorian and modern fairy-tales—a deterioration matched in religion by that sentimentality which mars much of the devotion, both Roman and Anglican, of the nineteenth century, in pictures and in hymns. This is the reduction of the *aweful* to the trivial, and the rejection of austerity and grandeur. MacDonald had a word to say about such religious art: "If the Lord were to appear this day in England as once in Palestine, he would not come in the halo of the painters or with that wintry shine of effeminate beauty or sweet weakness in which it is their helpless custom to depict him."

C. S. Lewis has declared his debt to MacDonald. For him the reading of *Phantastes* was more than an intellectual discovery: it brought a recovery from mental sickness, a *metanoia**. He found in it *goodness*. "I had been waist-deep in romanticism," he wrote, "and likely enough at any moment to flounder into darker and more evil forms, slithering down the steep descent which leads from the love of strangeness to that of eccentricity,

* Conversion or turning

4

and thence to that of perversity." In *Phantastes* he found a new kind of romance, "a sort of cool, morning innocence, a certain quality of death, good Death. . . What it eventually did for me was to convert, even to baptise (that was where death came in) my imagination." Baptism is one's sacramental death to sin and rebirth to God. The magic of water appears often in Celtic lore; for MacDonald it is the purifying, baptismal element. Sister Water is blessed. Water in the river and in the mill-pond was part of his happy country boyhood.

MacDonald's influence is apparent both in Lewis's adult fantasies, especially *Perelandra,* and in his Narnian chronicle. Lewis might be called MacDonald's spiritual son and heir. With that other great creator of myth of our own day, J. R. R. Tolkien, there is an affinity rather than an influence. Tolkien, too, has contempt for the tinsel-and-gauze creatures who clutter the garden and are merely "a sophisticated product of literary fancy". They are a form of self-defence invented by those who cannot face either the grandeur or the terror of the true fairy-tale.

These two writers of our own day accept grandeur, thus also accepting and admitting awe and even terror. These elements blend with their homeliness—their love of earth, of the common man, of animals and of all growing things. Lewis was Anglican and of the High Church tradition which used to be called Anglo-Catholic. Tolkien was Roman Catholic. In both, all that was kind and lovely in the old paganism, the ancient piety of hearth and fields and woods, has found a place, transmuted and sanctified, in their Christian fantasies. Even without a word of doctrine (and, in Tolkien, without any explicit Christian background or reference, in his world of hobbits and elves) they are, like MacDonald, transmitters of the Christian faith and ethos, of the sacramental sequel to the Incarnation, for the Incarnation lies in the heart and soul of their creative genius.

Lewis and Tolkien, like MacDonald, compel us to contemplate the splendid and the terrible, to feel awe as well as delight. They bring us excitement, beauty, rapture and mystery. Tolkien and Lewis also bring us laughter in which MacDonald may be admitted to have been defective.

There is a particular affinity between MacDonald and Tolkien in the shared quality of *northernness*—Celtic in MacDonald and Scandinavian in Tolkien. They share, too, a mythological sense of the inner life of trees—of trees being, like men, both good and evil. In *The Fellowship of the Ring*, the first volume of the trilogy, *The Lord of the Rings*, Tolkien's hobbits, Frodo, Sam, Merry and Pippin, fall into peril at the beginning of their journey. The two young hobbits, Merry and Pippin, are caught by the evil tree, the Willow, and are rescued by Tom Bombadil. Later in their quest they meet the great, powerful and benign tree-creatures, the Ents.

This wood-magic, for both good and evil, begins in MacDonald's *Phantastes*. Anados, like Dante, finds himself in *una selva oscura*. The trees grow more and more dense as Anados advances. "Ere long, their crowded stems barred the sunlight out, forming, as it were, a thick grating between me and the East." No Virgil comes to be his guide through the ultimate horrors, but a girl gathering flowers bids him, "Trust the Oak and the Elm and the great Beech. Take care of the Birch, for though she is honest she is too young not to be changeable. But shun the Ash and the Alder; for the Ash is an Ogre—you will know him by his thick fingers; and the Alder will smother you with her web of hair if you let her near you at night."

Anados comes into utter stillness, where no living creature appears and no bird sings: a stillness of sleep and of expectation. The trees hold mystery. In the tree-cottage he finds the old woman, mother of the girl he had met, and she tells him he has fairy blood in him. Without that, he could not have come so far. In her Anados perceives, for all the roughness of her face, "a something unusual . . . an expression that contrasted strangely with the form of her features." Her hands, too, though brown, are delicately formed. (The shape and feel of hands was to recur, more significantly, in *The Princess and Curdie*.) The woman is kind. She warns him of danger; she gives him food and shelter. The first of the mothers in MacDonald's tales, she is shadowy still, but has wisdom and benignity in her.

The symbol of the hand recurs in the story. An evil hand, large and distorted, "with thick knobs and lumps on the fingers", casts its shadow across the cottage window. It is the hand of the evil Ash. He cannot do harm to those in the cottage, however, for they are guarded by the Oaks that form the corner-posts of the house. But Anados must beware of him in the forest.

When Anados enters the dark wood, his way is lit and enlivened by the flower-fairies. This episode might have been mere whimsy, but it escapes that flaw by its brevity, and by stressing the kinship of living things. "The flowers die because the fairies go away"—the fairies do not disappear because the flowers die. "The flowers seem a sort of house for them, or outer bodies, which they can put on or off when they please. . . Whether all the flowers have fairies I cannot determine, any more than I can be sure whether all men and women have souls."

The gaiety is brief. The way through the woods leads to darkness and peril and suffering. It is a pilgrim's progress, an allegory without too obvious a presentation of vices and virtues, a journey through Purgatory which brings the traveller back to this life, this earth, after effecting a purgation.

Anados comes to a beech tree and finds a woman within, a beautiful woman, loving and sad and protective. She gives him a girdle of her hair which turns to leaves, healing and wholesome leaves.

He comes to a cave, a pleasant refuge with a spring of clear water and mossy stones. There he sees a block of alabaster and, in it, the form of a woman, whom he releases. But she floats, white-veiled, out of the cave. Later he thinks he finds her again, but it is an evil form, the witch transformed into an Alder tree, hollow, horrible. She tears from him his girdle of leaves. The Ash reappears. Anados is very near death.

Next he comes to a house where a woman, neither welcoming nor repellant, warns him not to open a certain door. It is the ancient prohibition of fairy-tale. But he does open the door, and from the dark cupboard emerges a shadow, his own shadow, which will follow him to the end, a dark, dreary companion.

This is the first token of MacDonald's preoccupation with shadows. In his later fairy-tales, however, shadows are not malignant or threatening. Their symbolism is vague. Can a clue for their intepretation be found in *Living Flame of Love*, a passage from St John of the Cross? "For a man to cast his shadow over another signifies that he protects him," we read there. The over-shadowing of the Most High is the supreme protection. God's shadow falls upon the Blessed Virgin as the Holy Spirit comes to her.

"Everything has and makes a shadow which corresponds to its nature and size. If the thing is dense and opaque it will make a dark and dense shadow, and if it is clearer and lighter it will make a lighter shadow. . . The shadow of death, then, will be

7

darkness, which in one sense deprives us of all things. . . The shadow of life will be light; if Divine, Divine light; if human, natural light. What then will be the shadow of beauty? It will be other beauty, of the nature and proportions of that beauty. So the shadow of strength will be other strength of the nature and quality of that strength. And the shadow of wisdom will be other wisdom or, more correctly, it will be the same beauty and the same strength and the same wisdom in shadow, wherein will be recognised the nature and proportions of which the shadow is cast."*

Anados is haunted, not protected, by his shadow. He is following the way of purgation which leads through death. But in the wonderful fairy-tale, *The Golden Key*, which seems to grow out of *Phantastes*, the shadows are good and lovely. However, of this, more in its place.

The journey of Anados is not altogether through peril and gloom. He reaches a lovely place, a stream which is joined by other streams to become a great river in a landscape which, he recalls, "glimmered in such bewitching loveliness that I felt as if I were entering Fairy Land for the first time." He is welcomed by loving hands and voices. Roses bloom everywhere—"they not only perfumed the air, they seemed to dye it a faint rose-hue." It has something of the radiance and colour of Purgatory as Dante ascends the mount and terraces of purification and meets the benign, rejoicing souls. But there is no Beatrice yet. Anados longs to see the woman of the Beech tree and the true woman of the statue, whose place was usurped by the evil Alder. A boat bears him along the river. He hears marvellous bird-song. The boat brings him to an enchanted palace which offers a good welcome. Invisible servants wait upon him; he sleeps in peace.

This is pure fairy-tale. The enchanted palace is bright with silver—a place of luminous beauty set amid gardens and lawns, bordered by wood and valley, lake and hill, with birds and beasts living their own lives therein. However, the shadow is still with him, though faint. This is not the end of the journey. Terror and ugliness lie ahead: there are goblins, malignant and hideous. This is the first appearance of those creatures who later attack the Princess and her father in MacDonald's great fairy-tale, *The Princess and the Goblin*. Indeed, the romance *Phantastes* is the source of nearly all MacDonald was to write for children.

* *The Living Flame of Love*, St John of the Cross, translated by E. Allison Peers, Doubleday Books, 1962, Stanza III.

Tolkien, nearly a hundred years later, was to tell an enchanting story, *The Hobbit,* from which grew his saga, *The Lord of the Rings.* In MacDonald the great fantasy is the source of the small enchantments.

Anados comes, in the end, to the final conflict. He finds again the lady of his love and her knight, and defends them, overthrowing the terrible creature that threatens all life. But in the conflict he himself is slain. The lady and the knight weep for him, but he is at peace. He knows that the victory has come, and the final purgation: "My spirit rejoiced. They left me to my repose. I felt as if a cool hand had been laid on my heart and had stilled it."

But from that dream-death he must awaken, in agony, and return to this mortality, to his own familiar country, his castle, his kindred. He wakens to see his haunting shadow, but as the sun comes up the shadow diminishes. It is no longer a monster of darkness, but simply a place where the sun does not shine. It is "only the natural shadow that goes with every man who walks in the sun".

He must now live in expectation. "I who had set out to find my Ideal, came back rejoicing that I had lost my Shadow." His journey through Purgatory has ended. "I know that good is coming to me—that good is always coming."

Chapter 2

THE MAKING OF THE MAKER

The Background of George MacDonald

Phantastes is the source of the fairy-tales. But beyond that book lies its own source—the genius of MacDonald, and his background, heredity and upbringing. The man and the maker cannot be separated, and the child is father of both.

George MacDonald was born in 1824 in the little country town of Huntly in Aberdeenshire. He did not come from the Celtic Highlands although his ancestry and heritage were Celtic. His father was a miller who also owned some farm fields. Family prosperity had diminished but there was no real poverty, only austerity, and a simplicity in material things is no bad training for a poet and story-teller.

MacDonald's was a happy childhood except for one profound grief, the death of his mother when he was eight years old. His father married again, however, and George and his brothers were given the kindest of stepmothers so that there was no lack of maternal care. But the memory of his own young mother haunts his tales as a gentle and benign presence which finds many incarnations, both fairy and human. There is often a good father as well, as in that loveliest of the tales, *At the Back of the North Wind,* or in the two *Princess* books, where Curdie's father, the miner, is strong and helpful. But the mother figure is more important. There are the human mothers of little Diamond and of Curdie; there is the great North Wind herself; and, most beautiful of all, there is the Queen-Grandmother. The North Wind is at once an elemental goddess and a powerful good angel. The Queen-Grandmother resembles the Queen of Heaven herself, the Mother of God, whom MacDonald showed veiled but whose influence is present. The mother, human or fairy, in MacDonald's books is what Beatrice is in *The Divine Comedy,* and behind her, reached through her, is Our Lady.

The mother figure comes into MacDonald's novels too—in Janet, the shepherd's wife in *Sir Gibbie;* in Kirsty, who, in

Ranald Bannerman's Boyhood[7], welcomes the boys, Ranald and his brothers, to her fireside and tells them wonderful legends, being herself a good Highlander. Only once, in *David Elginbrod*, does the father surpass the mother in tenderness and understanding. Margaret's mother, there, is completely good and kind, but her father has a special insight.

MacDonald's own father was loving and beloved, although, like many a Scots father of that generation, he was reserved and a strict disciplinarian—but that was accepted as natural and proper. The children knew security and protection, and they accepted authority. MacDonald later told his son Greville[8] that the character of David Elginbrod was drawn from his own father. Yet Robert Wolff, in his analytical biography, *The Golden Key*[9], cannot accept this. He insists upon a hidden resentment. A son, in his view, must resent his father, and if the father so far forgets his part as to be kind as well as authoritative, then "filial love makes the filial resentment all the more shameful".

More simply and reasonably, C. S. Lewis finds the father-son relationship in MacDonald's early life altogether happy, and quotes MacDonald's statement that, "Fatherhood must be at the core of the universe." He recalled for his son Greville many good memories of his boyhood, to which his stepmother had contributed. George and his brothers were trained in courtesy. They always rose to open the door for her and for their father; they picked up her dropped knitting wool and waited upon her. Rules were strict but their father knew when to relax them and when to ignore lapses. Disobedience was punished but escapades were often ignored.

The family lived very plainly. Clothes were worn to shabbiness, but this did not at all distress the boys. Food was plain but abundant and there were country delicacies such as "wild bees' nests in the stone dykes* whose honeycomb, eaten like bread, was a priceless joy."

School could be harsh. According to Greville MacDonald, the ferocious dominie in *Alec Forbes*[10], Murdoch Malison, had a living prototype. The schoolmaster in many a Scots village was a failed or "stickit" minister, embittered by frustration. In the novel he is granted "a divine repentance", and that too may have been true. MacDonald probably wrote from memory when he described Alec and his companions rushing out of school with

* Walls

11

shouts of joy because, "Every day to them was a cycle of strife, suffering and deliverance." The day began with prayers which revealed a world ruled by "the god of a corrupt Calvinism in the person of Murdoch Malison . . . not the God revealed in the Man Jesus Christ". After school the boys "went home to heaven for the night", and it is unlikely that they told their parents anything of what had happened in school.

The MacDonalds were country boys and, whatever they might have suffered in school, there were happy holidays during which they could enjoy the "pools for swimming and a river for boating" at Huntly. For George these offered a more than physical delight. All his life he loved running water with clear depths in which to plunge and be cleansed and cooled. His story *The Carasoyn* recalls this delight. Colin, the shepherd's son, makes the burn run through the cottage kitchen. One night he awakens to see the fairy fleet sailing along it. He hears a cry for help from a little girl, taken by the fairy queen, and he follows the fleet to rescue her.

MacDonald knew the water-magic of Celtic fairy-tales. This was not always an amiable magic. Kelpies are not benignant and neither are the creatures of the deep who may steal away a princess. Beyond MacDonald's boyish fun on the river lay an inherited memory of enchantment, its menace made delectable by the security of actual life.

For animals MacDonald had a Franciscan tenderness inherited from his father. The boys learned to ride bareback on the farm horses. Having proved that they could stay on, they were promoted to a saddle. Horses and dogs were childhood comrades and friends, with their own cherished personalities.

The boy, Diamond, in *At the Back of the North Wind* is named after a favourite horse. His father is a coachman and Diamond sleeps in the loft above the stable. He helps his father: he even drives a cab, and drives it well and steadily. Dogs and horses may lead the procession of MacDonald's animal friends, but all kinds of creatures are in it, and birds fly overhead. They all come into the fairy-tales as comrades and helpers of the hero or heroine, as they do in many of the old Celtic legends, where, between people and animals, there is kinship, mutual help and dependence, courtesy and gratitude. All such animals go to Paradise in the end, as a reward for their valour, loyalty and love. This doctrine did not endear MacDonald to those who had

12

doubts about the salvation of many men and women, let alone the beasts and birds.

Part of MacDonald's boyhood is reflected in *Alec Forbes*, and more, perhaps, in *Ranald Bannerman's Boyhood*, in which, although no marvels occur, there is magic in the tales told by Kirsty to Ranald and his brothers. They are the sons of the parish minister, a gentle scholar, elderly and a little remote, but, in his dealings with his boys, showing real sympathy. Their mother is dead and the housekeeper at the manse is a dragon of a woman. The mother figure is Kirsty, who keeps house for the men on the glebe or manse farm.

As a child, MacDonald created his own imaginary magic town within the real town of Huntly. Always he had a profound sense of kinship with the animals and with all created things. All of this is reflected in *Ranald Bannerman*, with its intense awareness of other-worldliness and of the essence of things. Published in 1871, in the same year as *At the Back of the North Wind*, this book is the bridge between the novels and the fairy-tales. It shows magic as a potential literary element.

In the book, Ranald recalls his dreams, "where or when dreamed, the Good One who made me only knows". In one dream, he found himself in his own room, but it had become higher. The window had gone and in the ceiling had appeared the sun, moon and stars. The sun was like that in a penny picture book, "a round, jolly, jocund man's face"; the moon was "such a one as you may see with the cow jumping over". The moon looked trustfully at the sun, he merrily at her. "The stars were their children . . . and they seemed to run about the ceiling. . . I have vague memories of having heard their talk," Ranald recalls. In one corner of the room there seemed to be a ladder of sun-rays. This the dreamer tried to climb, but at first his feet kept slipping back. Then one night he did climb it, up and up, with a soft wind blowing about him, made, he thought in his dream, of kisses from his dead baby brother. "I began to weep for very delight of something I have forgotten," he remembers, and then he awoke, sobbing. Here we have the germ of the vision, to appear later in *The Princess and the Goblin*, of the moon-lamp, high in the tower, which guides the way to the Queen in her room.

Some time later Ranald, now grown older, is shown coming out of school into the warm sun. He sat "in perfect bliss upon the earthen walls which divided the fields from the road, and basked in the heat", absorbing the warmth and scent and view. In the manse garden he could see guelder roses hang "like balls of snow in their wilderness of green leaves, and here and there the damask roses, dark almost to blackness". The rose haunted MacDonald's imagination with more than beauty of scent and colour. His son recalled words spoken half aloud, half to the speaker himself in meditation: "The rose, when it gives some glimmer of the freedom for which a man hungers, does so because of its substantial unity with the man, each in its own degree being a signature of God's immanance. To a spiritual pilgrim the flower no longer seems a pretty design on the wall . . . she opens the wicket into the land of poetic reality, and he, passing through and looking gratefully back, then knows her for his sister the Rose, of spiritual substance one with him. . . So also we may find co-substance between the stairs of a cathedral and our own secret stair up to the vision of God." Stairs were another beloved symbol. The land of poetic reality is MacDonald's country.

Ranald and his brothers find Kirsty "our constant resort . . . our refuge in all times of trouble and necessity." She will bind up cut fingers, welcome them to her fireside and tell them tales. She is from "a region where the hills were hills indeed, hills with mighty skeletons of stone inside them; hills that looked as if they had been heaped over huge monsters which were ever trying to get up, a country where every cliff and rock and well had its story." We have no glimpse of such a landscape again until we find it in Tolkien. These legends which Kirsty told to the boys were part of MacDonald's heritage too.

One of the tales is of a knight whose effigy lies on a tomb in the parish church, close to the manse pew. It is an ancient church which has "seen candles burning, heard the little bell ringing, and smelt the incense of the old Catholic service. It was so old that it seemed settling down again into the earth."

MacDonald himself did not worship in such an ancient church, but his heritage of the old faith was not remote. His great-grandfather had been a Catholic (and a Jacobite who fought at Culloden). The old sacramental faith was in his bones, not to be driven out by the Calvinism of more immediate forebears. One of MacDonald's grandmothers was a strict Calvinist, and she was the prototype of the grandmother of

14

Robert Falconer in the novel of that name. Her hatred of Catholicism was slightly mellowed by natural kindness and the pity she felt for its misguided adherents, even for the Pope himself. As a very old woman she read in the newspapers of the election of Pius IX, the liberal Pope—as so many, both Catholic and Protestant, hoped to find him. The old woman remarked, "The newspaper is telling that amang a' the changes takin' place in the warld, they have gotten a guid Pope at Rome; and I have been prayin' to the Lord a' nicht to gi'e him a new he'rt and a guid wife."

From school MacDonald went to King's College, Aberdeen, a poor student. Like many another, he took a post as tutor during the long vacation. This was in a castle with a great library such as he had never seen before, and with many stairs leading to fine rooms and to attics. This real castle was later transmuted by MacDonald into that of the *Princess*. It became poetry:

> The house is not for me, it is for Him.
> His royal thoughts require many a stair,
> Many a tower, many an outlook fair
> Of which I have no thought.

May there not be another echo here of St John of the Cross, of his great poem, *The Dark Night of the Soul?*

> In safety, in disguise
> In darkness, up the secret stair I crept.*

Having graduated from Aberdeen, MacDonald went south to one of the theological colleges of the Congregational Church, entered that ministry and was appointed to a charge in Arundel. There he offended his congregation by preaching the love and fatherhood of God in a measure far beyond their approval.

Dismissed from his charge, he went with his wife and first child to Manchester, where he found varied work but experienced financial uncertainty. He wrote for a journal, *The Christian Spectator*, he preached to a small congregation which met in "a preaching room", he gave lectures and held classes in the new Ladies' College: there was plenty of work, and all of it congenial, but it brought in too little money for an increasing family. Mercifully he found benefactors, among them Lady Byron, who sent him and his wife to Algiers after an illness which had brought him very near death.

Soon afterwards came his appointment as a lecturer at King's

* From *Poems of St John of the Cross*, translated by Roy Campbell, Harvill Press.

15

College, London, and he and his family settled in London. In 1854 he published his poem *Within and Without,* reviewed in *The Scotsman* as being "full of the most exquisite poetry . . . a very remarkable production of intellect and heart united as perhaps they seldom have been before." *Phantastes* followed, then a series of novels (the first, *David Elginbrod,* in 1863), then his *Dealings with the Fairies* and his three great books for children, *At the Back of the North Wind, The Princess and the Goblin* and *The Princess and Curdie.*

By this time he was well established as a man of letters, with many friends including Lewis Carroll, F. D. Maurice (who had helped him to his post at King's College and brought him into the Church of England) and Arthur Hughes, the artist, a sympathetic illustrator of his tales. Had MacDonald taken Holy Orders, he would have produced fewer books; there would have been less time for writing. But the Church would have gained a priest spiritually akin to George Herbert.

In 1865 he was a candidate for the Chair of Rhetoric and Belles Lettres (now known as that of English Literature) at Edinburgh University. Other candidates included that great and delightful scholar, David Masson, who was the one appointed. MacDonald's son Greville has suggested that the novel *David Elginbrod* was held against his father by some of the godly, who especially objected to the epitaph shown by David to the young hero, Hugh:

Here lie I, Martin Elginbrod.
Have mercy on my soul, Lord God,
As I would do were I Lord God,
And Thou wert Martin Elginbrod.

The stability and honour of such an academic appointment would indeed have been desirable, but MacDonald's disappointment was tempered by his realisation that the east winds and *haar* of Edinburgh winters would have been a danger to him. Even London was to prove trying to his health.

The MacDonalds lived at Hammersmith in the house then called the Retreat, which was later to be bought by William Morris and renamed Kelmscott House. It was a large house with ample room for his eleven children and frequent guests. It had a wide garden, stables and a stable yard, where a walnut tree grew. A tulip tree grew on the lawn, and in the shrubbery stood a statue of Artemis with a stag. A road ran between garden and river; it was almost a private walk. The family found the house delightful. Morris, when he bought it in 1878, took a more critical view. His first biographer, J. W. Mackail, son-in-law of Edward Burne-Jones, has described the house as "ugly without being mean", with the river so near as sometimes to overflow the wall and flood the cellars. (This might have suggested to MacDonald the goblins' attack on the castle in *The Princess and the Goblin*.)

Many guests came to the Retreat, and one of young Greville's high memories was of going out to call a cab for Tennyson. The parents found their "serviceable children" worth double their number in servants. They once helped to entertain guests by acting a dramatised version of *The Pilgrim's Progress* produced by their mother.

Authors, clergy, artists (the Burne-Joneses among them) and social workers all came to visit. Among these last were Canon Barnett, founder of Toynbee Hall, and Octavia Hill, who brought some of her poor proteges with her. A pioneer in slum clearance, she would buy some of the most dilapidated houses in a poor area, make them decent and then let them to tenants of whom few had immaculate records. All was forgiven them provided they paid their rents, which were never high and most of which were spent by her on repairs and sanitation. She also found work for her tenants. From her and from Canon Barnett, MacDonald heard first-hand accounts of London's poor. He was moved to a compassion which at times came near despair. This awareness of poverty lurks in the background of *North Wind*, although Diamond's parents never descend to utter poverty, and are of the highest decency and integrity.

The Retreat was sold in 1878. Much of MacDonald's later life was spent in Italy, at Bordigherra, in a house named *Casa Coraggio*, which friends had helped him to buy. Both he and his wife lived into the new century, she dying in 1902, MacDonald in 1905, he, in his last years, being clouded in mind.

17

Chapter 3

MAGIC JOURNEYS

MacDonald's Fairy-Tales for Children

C. S. Lewis has said that a writer may be mastered by the dominant literary form of his period. This form in the nineteenth century was the novel. For many writers it was the natural vehicle, but not for MacDonald. He was essentially a teller of magic tales, a poet, a maker of myth. His peculiar genius gleams fitfully in his novels, shining most clearly and steadily when he writes of boyhood and the country, recalling and evoking his own youth, as in the early chapters of *Alec Forbes, Robert Falconer* and *Sir Gibbie*. In Gibbie the child there is something of Diamond. Gibbie, the small dumb waif escaping from the city to wander among the hills of his own lost inheritance, has innocence and a touch of magic. As a grown-up hero he is less convincing. Had these novels ended with boyhood they would have been altogether delightful, even if they had failed to satisfy a public addicted to the three-decker novel.

In *Ranald Bannerman* there are many hints of the fairy-tales to come, a clear prelude to fairy music: "I cannot recall the memory of these summer days without a gush of delight gurgling over my heart, just as the water used to gurgle over the stones of the dam. . . For innocent animal delight I know nothing to match these days so warm yet so pure-aired, so clean and glad. I often think how God must love His little children to have invented for them such delights."

These were summer days, but winter had its own memories. Ranald recalls a long ride with his father through a desolate landscape, sunless and deep in snow. His father tells him, "Of all material things the sun is likest to God. If you turn your face to the sun, my boy, your soul will, when you come to die, feel like an autumn with all the golden fruits of the earth hanging in rich clusters, ready to be gathered. . . You will die in peace, hoping for the spring—and such a spring."

The picture is more like Italy than the north, and the teaching more akin to that of St Francis, who praised Brother Sun, than to the usual Scots sermon.

At the Back of the North Wind takes up all the hints of enchantment and plays the full fairy music. Diamond, like Ranald, loves horses. His father is coachman to a wealthy family and he lives in the mews and sleeps in the hayloft above the stall of the horse whose name he shares. "There was hay at his feet and hay at his head, all piled up in great trusses to the very roof," and "a little lane with several turnings" between the bales. Going to bed was a tiny journey. The description must have thrilled many a child in a stuffy nursery and no doubt it shocked many a nurse. Diamond, undressed by his mother in her room, wanders off by himself along the lanes between the trusses, lingering a little by the way, then shooting into his warm bed, snuggling down and thinking "what a happy boy he was". He can hear the other Diamond below in his stall.

And one night a visitor comes. At first she is a little frightening, somewhat stern and reproving. It is the North Wind herself. "Her dark eyes looked a little angry for they had just begun to flash; but a quivering in her sweet upper lip made her look as if she were going to cry. . . The darkness in the hayloft looked as if it were made of her hair. . . The boy was entranced with her mighty beauty. . . From her eyes came all the light by which Diamond saw her face and her hair."

The North Wind reassures him, she knows his mother, saying, "I was with her when you were born."

His first flight at the back of the North Wind, hidden in a nest of her dark hair, carries him to central London and leaves him in a poor street, talking to a girl, Nanny, a wretched little scrap of a crossing-sweeper, but a tough little scrap, too. MacDonald may himself have known such children and understood their background, and he certainly heard of them from Octavia Hill. The two wander on together, and the adventure ends with Diamond finding himself at home, at the garden door of his master's house.

Thereafter come many more journeys and many marvels of discovery. The North Wind grows more and more benign, more beautiful and maternal. Greville MacDonald has said that this was the most continuously popular of his father's books for children, the secret is its "two-world consciousness", the symbolism being so lovely, so gossamer light, that it drifts into the mind. The author, carried off on a strong wind of inspiration, carried the children with him.

There was also, for contemporary readers, the charm of a familiar setting. Many of them knew just such a large house, with garden and stable-loft, as he describes, and which was similar to his own London home. Many of them knew about crossing-sweepers and other poor children from various improving books for the young. This realism made the enchantment of Diamond's adventures the more convincing.

MacDonald could, in his son's words, make "an appeal to the imaginative seeing of a truth" because he himself saw truth and goodness through his poetic imagination, and not dimmed by it but made more clear. In this light he saw and conveyed the Gospel. He saw into the heart of creation and into the hearts of children.

"My father's knowledge of what food children best thrive upon", wrote Greville MacDonald, "came from his own child-like faith in their celestial inheritance," which was much more than a sentimental view of childish virtue. "True feeding of the child is more subtle a thing than psychologists can fathom. George MacDonald did fathom it and in a way that was absolutely matchless. . . Magic and mystery, nonsense and fun did more for us than moral precept or standardised education. *North Wind* is full of light, renewing itself to this day."

MacDonald was, after all, "a numerous parent", likely to know something about children of all ages. He knew in his own childhood, and gave to his own children, a happy background, with security and stability rather than material wealth. In Diamond's experience, the same sort of steady background survives even under the threat of poverty. His parents are steadfast and good, his father protective, his mother infinitely tender and understanding. Although Diamond did not tell her about his first adventure, he "had half a notion that North Wind was a friend of his mother's and that, if she did not know *all* about it, at least she did not mind his going anywhere with the lady of the wind."

Diamond's father loses his job when his master loses his fortune. He sets up for himself as a cabman and Diamond helps him, even in driving the cab. After an illness, he is sent for convalescence to an aunt in Sandwich, a "sleepy old town . . .

nearly dead of old age . . . a town abandoned by its nurse the sea." The North Wind comes to him still and their flights take him further and further into the country "at the back of the North Wind" where other travellers have gone, long ago, beyond time and space. Kilmeny went there in the Ettrick Shepherd's poem, to that land "where the cock never crew and the wind never blew"; Dante ascended there, from Hell into Purgatory.

In this episode Diamond goes "far ben", in the good Scots phrase, into the land of stillness and "a certain rayless light". It is near Paradise, yet it is not wholly Paradise. It is a place of expectancy rather than fulfilment or bliss. But it is not Purgatory either, for Diamond is too innocent to need purging from sin. And Dante's Purgatory is, unlike Diamond's land of stillness, a region of light and colour, radiance and activity. The souls there are joyful and humble, accepting their time of waiting and expiation as a gift from God to prepare them for the unutterable bliss of Paradise.

Diamond cannot be perfectly happy there because his mother and father are not with him, but he feels "so still and quiet and patient and contended that it was something better than mere happiness. Nothing went wrong at the back of the north wind. Neither was anything quite right, either, he thought. Only everything was going to be right some day." It is easy to see this place as that of the expectant and peaceful dead, purged of their sins, less active and joyful than those in Dante's Purgatory, but awaiting, in hope and patience, their summons to God's nearer Presence.

From this visionary episode, the tale brings Diamond back to London to find a new baby brother, whom he dearly cherishes. The family fortunes begin to mend. Diamond meets a good friend in his cab-driving, a wealthy man who takes them all to his house in the country, making Diamond's father his coachman. It is the setting they all love. He takes care, also, of Nanny, the crossing-sweeper.

For a time the North Wind has been absent. The enchantment has been withdrawn. Everyday life itself is good. Then she returns as a strong angel summoning Diamond away. He makes one more journey with her, and in the morning he cannot be wakened. "They thought he was dead. I knew that he had gone to the back of the north wind."

21

There is nothing here of the tear-drenched Dickensian deathbeds of Little Nell or Paul Dombey. There is no sentimentality, simply statement. Diamond's death is inevitable, like the departure of Kilmeny in Hogg's poem: this world "wasna her hame, and she couldna remain". Diamond, too, is of the company of the holy innocents.

Reading *At the Back of the North Wind* can be more than an adventure or a discovery: it can be a turning point. It can be a *metanoia*. In this story we are in a new dimension. It is different even from MacDonald's other enchantments, although there is a hint of it in *The Shadows* and in *The Golden Key*. And with that change in dimension there goes the realism of the setting. MacDonald's fairy tales and his two *Princess* books are set in faerie itself, or in its borderland, or in some kingdom of legend where once upon a time marvels occurred. But the North Wind comes to Diamond in the stable-loft of a house on the outskirts of London. He is carried to the poor streets of the city—any London child would know the background and children elsewhere would not find it strange. This blend of realism and fantasy makes the book unique in MacDonald's work.

Yet it is a familiar device within the Celtic tradition. The king or princess in many a Celtic tale passes, in a moment of time, from the familiar scene into faerie. MacDonald cannot be fully understood or valued without a knowledge of his inheritance.

MacDonald's collection of stories, *Dealings with the Fairies*, which preceded *North Wind* in date, being published in 1868, has the same quality and shares the same ancestry. In the story *The Carasoyn*, there is a queen who is, if not wholly malignant, certainly selfish and demanding. She carries off a human child, asking as ransom a bottle of carasoyn or magic wine. The hero Colin resists her and, after many adventures, wins the little girl back.

In another of the stories, *The Shadows*, a good man, Ralph Rinkelmann, is chosen as king of the fairies after their democratic manner, but he is visited in a grave illness by the Shadows, who claim him as their king, too, and desire him to visit their land. This is in the far north under ice and snow: its remote northernness is stressed. The Shadows, however, are far from evil. They are not like the black figure of menace which follows Anados in *Phantastes*. They have their own laws and loyalties; they can be benevolent, like the shadow that plays

22

with a sick and lonely little boy. They appear "tall and solemn rather than awful". They tell their king something about their nature: "We do not belong to the sunshine at all, we go through it unseen." But the darkness is not evil. There is a dialogue between the king and the chief of the Shadows in which the king asks:

Can that be true that loves the night?

He is answered with:

—The darkness is the nurse of light.
Can that be true which mocks at forms?
—Truth rides abroad in shapeless storms.

The shadow theme recurs in another story, *The Golden Key*. Again we remember St John of the Cross. Here the shadows are good: they fall from a place of light. The tale begins enticingly, showing the small hero, Mossy (so called because he sits reading so long upon a mossy stone), living with his great-aunt in a little house on the borders of fairyland. She tells him marvellous tales, tells him about the golden key which lies at the foot of the rainbow. The forest outside his window begins to summon him (but without the menace that lurked for Anados) "as if all the trees were waiting for him, and had something they could not go on with until he came." Mossy obeys their call. At the end of an aisle of trees he sees a rainbow shining in colours more glorious than any he had ever seen. And so he begins his journey and quest for the rainbow. The rainbow, when he reaches it, is more than a spectrum of colours. Within it appear "beautiful forms slowly ascending as if by steps of a winding stair".

Mossy meets a companion at the beginning of his journey—a little girl nicknamed Tangle because of her ill-brushed hair. She is the only child of a wealthy but neglectful father. Her mother is dead and there is no-one to care for her. The servants in her father's house are callous and careless. So Tangle runs away. She is guided to a cottage in the forest where a beautiful lady welcomes her, bathes her, dresses her in a fine green gown and, after supper, puts her to bed in a green arbour on a bed of purple heath, covered with a sheet of feathers. All the next day Tangle spends in the forest, listening happily to the talk of the birds and beasts which she can understand perfectly. They are comical creatures, giving each other a good deal of amicable backchat. The mole tells the squirrel that his tail is the best part of him; the squirrel retorts by calling the mole "old spade-fists".

Mossy comes to the cottage. He has the golden key, found at the foot of the rainbow, although he does not know what door it will open. The lady of the cottage bids him take Tangle with him on his quest for the door.

Their journey begins gaily. They are amused by the talk of the forest creatures who are friendly and helpful. The squirrel brings them nuts and the moles bring earth-nuts or truffles. There is a gaiety which is not too frequent in MacDonald's fairy-tales. It has something of the quality of *The Wind in the Willows*. MacDonald could probably have written a delightful book entirely about animals in their own kingdom. He knew what St John of the Cross calls "the great delight of this awakening [to God]: to know the creatures through God and not God through the creatures."

This happiness for Mossy and Tangle is brief. They lie down to sleep "in the heart of a heap of shadows" and Tangle awakes to find herself alone. She must go on by herself, as did the sad heroine in the old legend *The Black Bull of Norroway*, who had, through brief forgetfulness, disobeyed an injunction not to move hand or foot. Tangle is not even guilty of forgetfulness: she has had no warning or command. Fate simply declares that she and Mossy must go the rest of the journey by separate ways. And it is a long journey.

Tangle meets the three Old Men of Earth and Sea and Fire. Only the Old Man of the Fire can help her, although all are benevolent. He first appears as a child in a cave. There is "something in her knowledge which was not in her understanding" which prepares Tangle for the change and revelation. The child "had no smile, but the love in his large grey eyes was as deep as the centre . . . the heart of the child was too deep for any smile to reach from it to his face." The Child-Man sends Tangle to the country whence the shadows fall, there to await Mossy.

He in his turn wanders for many years until, old and grey, he comes to the Old Man of the Sea, who bathes him in water which renews his youth and strength. It is a symbolic baptism and rebirth. Across a dark sea he comes to the foot of the rainbow again, climbs a high rock and finds there a tiny keyhole. This opens to his golden key. A door in the rock reveals a stair leading up into a hall of pillars where Tangle is awaiting him. She too had grown old and grey, but is now renewed, becoming tall and noble and lovely. In that hall she has waited seven years for Mossy, in the way that the heroine of *The Black Bull of Norroway* served seven years before she could find her lost love. Tangle and Mossy tell each other all their adventures.

The hall grows dark, then glimmers with light. Mossy sees that one of the pillars is luminous with that marvellous colour he had discovered, so long ago, in the rainbow in the forest. In this pillar is another tiny stair. They climb together, up and up within the rainbow, within its colour and luminance, looking through its transparent walls upon the earth far below. "Stairs upon stairs wound up together, and beautiful beings of all ages climbed along with them. They knew they were going up to the country whence the shadows fall. And by this time I think they must have got there."

The shadows referred to here are wholly good and lovely. They are the shadows and images of light and truth, shadows of the Godhead, shadows of all that men can see in this life which leads him into immortality.

There are symbolic stairs again in *The Princess and the Goblin*. These are also real stairs, stairs in a castle such as MacDonald had seen and remembered in his youthful days as tutor. Here the symbolism is explicit. The stairs are both real and paradisal. The strange magic journey is contained in a familiar setting, a device to be followed by other writers for children with entrancing results.

In the same year as *The Princess and the Goblin*, 1872, appeared *Alice in Wonderland*. Lewis Carroll was a friend of MacDonald and read the story to the MacDonald children, who applauded and encouraged him. Alice is out of doors when the wonders begin, but in the sequel, *Alice through the Looking-Glass*, she is in her mother's drawing-room. She climbs on to the chimney-piece and goes through the looking-glass into a fantastic world. The magic here is intellectual, comic and ironic, of a different quality from that of MacDonald. The coincidence in time of the two creations is, however, fascinating. Brightness had returned to the air of children's literature. The magic casements were wide open.

MacDonald's story, *The Princess and the Goblin*, begins on a wet day. The little Princess Irene is bored and miserable, "not knowing what she would like except it were to go out and get thoroughly wet, and catch a particularly nice cold and have to go to bed and take gruel," a mood familiar in many a nursery which, in a moral tale, would have led to mischief followed by punishment. MacDonald knew better. He opened the nursery door on "a curious old stair of worm-eaten oak which looked as if never anyone had set foot upon it." Irene sets her foot there (she had once climbed a few steps but no further) and climbs up and up to a long passage with many doors leading into other passages with more doors and many turnings, until she begins to feel a little afraid. Meanwhile the rain makes "a great trampling noise upon the roof". She turns back, turns again and again, and feels lost and terrified. "It doesn't follow that she was lost because she had lost herself, though," points out MacDonald.

After crying for a little, she goes bravely on like a true princess, coming to another stair, a tiny, narrow one which she must climb on hands and knees. At the top she hears a sound like "the humming of a happy bee that has found a rich well of honey". The sound leads her to a room where a lady sits spinning—not an old witch like the one who sent that other fairy-tale princess to sleep for a hundred years, but a queenly woman, her face smooth as a girl's although her long hair is white. Her eyes are very old, very wise and very kind.

"I am your father's mother's father's mother," she tells Irene, who replies composedly and courteously, "Then you are a Queen." Irene remains very much the Princess in this sedate courtesy. Like Alice in both her wonderlands, she is always the well-trained, well-mannered Victorian child.

The Queen, in her ageless beauty, her strength and gentleness, and her benign wisdom, is guardian of the kingdom and, especially, of the royal family. She is the fairy-godmother of legend, but transmuted, in that her magic power is radiant with holiness. She is, indeed, as G. K. Chesterton first pointed out, a figure of Our Lady. MacDonald may deliberately have cloaked and veiled the religious figure in fairy-tale queenliness, or he may have been only half aware himself of the true significance of his Queen and may have been fulfilling a profound, half-realised need in himself when clothing her in holiness. The Queen is the greatest and loveliest of all the mother figures—wise woman, nurse, or North Wind—who appear in his stories.

This first meeting between Irene and the Queen is brief. When

Irene returns to her nursery she finds her nurse anxious and reproachful and her story is not believed. She herself begins to doubt its reality. An attempt to rediscover the Queen in her attic leads to neither sound nor sight of her, and the Princess must come downstairs again, down, this time, to the kitchen where she is welcomed and petted by the servants. Magic cannot be compelled. The Queen will appear only when she chooses and it is she who will summon Irene.

The next adventure occurs out of doors. Irene is lost with her somewhat dim-witted nurse on the mountain beyond the castle. They are surrounded by malicious, mocking goblins and are rescued by Curdie, the miner's son. (In an old fairy-tale his father would have been a woodman or a charcoal-burner.) Curdie drives away the goblins with a rude but effective song:

> There's a toad
> In the road!
> Smash it,
> Squash it,
> Fry it!
> Dry it!
> You're another!
> Up and off!
> There's enough! Huuuh!

The Princess and her nurse reach home safely. Curdie spends that night in the mine, to overhear the goblins' plot to overthrow the castle by tunnelling underneath it. The King, hearing of the danger, rides home on his white horse. He listens uneasily to an account of the adventure, but he must ride back to his capital where other dangers threaten.

The little Princess again finds the Queen-Grandmother. She is sitting in the moonlight, her hair silvery in its luminance. She is spinning a ball of fine, silvery thread. Irene is cherished and put to bed in the Queen's own room, lit by a lamp like the moon, which never goes out. The Queen tells her about the pigeons which are her messengers. "In the darkest night", she says, "they always see my moon and know where to fly. . . If that light were to go out you would find yourself lying in a bare garret, on a heap of old straw." Irene falls asleep, and awakens in her own room.

There comes a night when, to escape an invading, pursuing goblin, Irene flees out of the castle and up the mountain, there to see the moon-lamp and follow its light safely to the Queen's bright room. She finds her transformed. She is even lovelier than before, young and golden-haired, robed in blue and crowned with silver and gems, her shoes covered with pearls and opals "glimmering like the Milky Way".

The Queen sits by a fire which burns with rose-flames. With them she touches her blue gown, soiled by Irene's muddy frock, for the child had fallen on the mountain-side. The stains vanish. Irene begs such cleansing for herself, but is told, "It is too hot for you yet, it would set your frock in flame."

There are gifts for Irene: a ring set with a fire-opal and a ball of the newly-spun silver thread. The thread is laid in a drawer and one end is fastened invisibly to the ring. "It would not be yours if it did not lie in my cabinet," explains the Queen. "If ever you find yourself in any danger . . . take off your ring and put it under the pillow of your bed. Then lay your forefinger upon the thread, and follow wherever it leads you." Is this, symbolically, the thread of prayer? Is it an emblem, unrealised by MacDonald himself, of the rosary?

The silver thread does indeed lead the Princess to safety, and with her Curdie, who, deep underground, has encountered the goblins in all their malignant power and is held captive. Irene feels a tug from the thread and lets it guide her—not up to the Queen's room but down to the caverns where Curdie is immured. She sets him free and they come up together, up the secret stair to the Lady, whom Irene sees, robed in white, sitting by her fire of flame-roses. But Curdie sees only a bare garret, a tub, a heap of straw, a withered apple "and a ray of sunlight coming through a hole in the middle of the roof".

He is not yet able to believe in certain things. "Seeing is not believing," the Lady tells Irene, "it is only seeing." Curdie's mother, who is good and gentle and wise, believes without seeing. Once she, too, had been beset by the goblins on the mountain, but, at the shining of a great moon-lamp, they had fled.

The Princess, pursued by the goblins, takes refuge in Curdie's cottage to be welcomed by his mother, and when the goblins make their last desperate attack upon the castle, from underground, they are repelled and defeated by Curdie, his father and the other miners. The castle is flooded and most of the evil creatures are drowned. The King takes Irene away to his palace in the city. He would like to have taken Curdie too, but Curdie chooses to stay with his parents. One reward he begs: a warm red petticoat for his mother.

The Princess and Curdie, published more than ten years later, is Curdie's story rather than Irene's. They have not met again. She is with her father in the city. Things are going ill with the kingdom: there are rumours of treachery. Curdie is now a grown youth working with his father in the mines. He is by no means bad or wild. He is not undutiful. But he has become difficult, going through the morose stage of adolescence, and his mother and father were "neither of them ready to sing when the thought of him came up".

One evening Curdie shoots a white pigeon. As it dies, it looks at him, and in a flash of compunction he realises all he has ignored and left undone: he feels true compassion and contrition. "Not till this very moment had he ever known what a pigeon was," or realised its joy in living. He thinks of the Princess and how they saved each other from peril. Now "he had stopped saving and begun killing".

The love of all creatures, so strong in MacDonald himself, is awakened in Curdie. Chesterton found the phrase for this quality in MacDonald when he called him "The Franciscan of Aberdeen".

There are more echoes of Dante in this story. When Curdie sees the moon-lamp high in the castle tower and follows its light up to the Queen's room, he is received by her as Dante is by Beatrice in Purgatory, with reproof. As he goes up the stairs, he hears the sound of spinning. A gentle voice bids him enter, but its very gentleness makes him tremble. He sees a tiny old woman, "so old that no age would have been too great to write under her picture", and looks at her, "a good deal in wonder, a very little in reverence, a little in doubt . . . a little in amusement", until he meets her eyes. Then "all the laugh went out of him".

The chiding is gentle but effective. "I am glad you shot my bird," she tells him. Glad, because the incident has brought about his awakening. Then she brings the pigeon back to life, holding it at her breast, its wings outspread "like a great mystical ornament of frosted silver". The woman is still old, but she has grown tall and queenly.

Then the light vanishes, and Curdie must grope his way out

of the dark room, down the stairs and home. He begs his mother's pardon for being late for supper. "There was something in the tone beyond the politeness that went to her heart, for it seemed to come from the place where all lovely things were born before they began to grow in this world." His parents know that something has happened. When Curdie tells them his adventure they believe it all and are glad.

Again he is drawn to the Queen's room and sees her spinning-wheel as a wheel of light, singing as it whirls, while she sings to its music. This is Dantesque. Curdie sees her now as a queen: tall, beautiful, ageless, robed in blue and crowned with silver and pearls. The attic is large and splendid. "The lofty ceiling was all a golden vine . . . and in its centre hung the most glorious lamp that human eyes ever saw—the silver moon itself . . . with a heart of light." In the hearth burns the fire of rose-flames. Into this Curdie is bidden to thrust his hands. He "dared not stop to think, it was much too terrible to think about." The pain is frightful but he endures it, holding it "as if it were a thing that would kill him if he let it go". At the height of the agony it diminishes and ends, leaving his hands unscarred but with the rough skin burned away. To the new smoothness and fineness an extra sense of touch has been added. The Queen tells him that he can now feel the nature of people by their hands. He will be able to sense that some are beasts or reptiles under their humanity. This will warn him of danger and thus be a means of defence.

The lady summons a creature called Lina who is part dog and of a fantastic ugliness, with elephant's legs, a head "something between that of a polar bear and a snake" and terrible fangs. Lina is bidden to offer a paw, which Curdie takes, trembling. He feels the soft hand of a child.

"Your gift does more for you than I promised," the Queen tells him benignly. "It is yet better to perceive a hidden good than a hidden evil." When he goes home, Curdie finds another hidden good which does not at all surprise him. Taking his mother's hand, which is rough, scarred and worn with work, he exclaims, "Mother, your hand feels just like that of the Princess." His mother is truly royal in grace of mind and personality, queenly in kindness.

Curdie must now go to the King. He is now ready for such service, and is needed. Lina follows him as guard. It is never told precisely who or what she is in her true self, but it is clear that she was once a woman who has now been expiating some sin, and that she is near the end of her expiation. For Curdie she is the most valiant and loyal of comrades. Like the dog, the otter, the eagle and other creatures in Celtic legend, she has been sent to help this human hero.

They come to the city of Gwyntystorm where the King lies ill, helpless and hopeless, surrounded by traitors. Princess Irene is alone, unbefriended and almost in despair. In the town itself Curdie is attacked, but he has other defenders now, a host of grotesque animals who have suddenly appeared and who follow him under the lead of Lina. "A strange torrent of deformity", they are a strong army. Curdie has made two human friends, also: a child who pats Lina and who, "by a right bountiful stretch of courtesy", calls her "doggy", and the child's grandmother, who is suspected of withcraft but who is kind and welcoming to Curdie. Within the palace he finds another true friend in a housemaid who looks after the sick King and the Princess.

Curdie can tell the nature of the traitors from their hands: they are reptiles and not human beings. The Princess welcomes him with great joy and is kind to Lina, caressing her with words and touch. The conflict begins between the horde of evil courtiers and the tiny group of the faithful. It is a conflict more subtle and terrifying even than the attack, years before, of the goblins. But it ends in victory. And, with victory, comes the Queen. Strong and radiant, she heaps her rose-flames about the King, restoring him to health and kingliness.

The last of those purging, healing flames is seen by the Princess. The Queen sits in her room, tending the fire. Lina lies before it, humble and expectant. The Queen gives the word and Lina passes joyfully into the heart of the flames. In her end is her beginning, her rebirth. We are told that now she has expiated every sin of her human life, that she is alive, free, joyful, her true self.

Even more clearly than its predecessor, *The Princess and Curdie* has echoes and undertones of Catholic and mystical music. The two books almost make a *Divine Comedy*. They show the Inferno of evil-doers condemned by their own acts, by their will to evil. They show the Purgatory of cleansing and suffering for those who, in spite of all their erring, have set their wills towards God. There is also a gleam of Paradise in the eucharistic feast at the end.

In the sound tradition of fairy-tale, the King gives his daughter in marriage to their rescuer, the brave Curdie. They all sit down to feast together, the King, the Princess and Curdie, a brave and faithful knight, the kind old woman and her grand-daughter (MacDonald can be trusted to remember a child). The good housemaid waits on them, pouring their wine. "As she poured out for Curdie red wine that foamed in the cup as if glad to see the light whence it had been banished so long, she looked him in the eyes, and Curdie sprang from his feet and dropped on his knees, and burst into tears"—for she is the Queen. She goes out, and returns robed in velvet and crowned with jewels, royal and glorious. The King and all his company kneel in homage. "But she made them all sit down, and in ruby crown and royal purple she served them all."

That lovely sentence should have been the end. Many a tale has ended with such a feast. In a usual fairy-tale the prince and princess would have lived happily ever after and would have ruled their kingdom wisely and well. Curdie and Irene are indeed happy in their marriage and wise and good in their rule, but they have no children. When they die, the people choose a new King who is base and unworthy. Greed infests the kingdom like a plague. In a mad search for gold, the people undermine the foundations of the city and it falls in ruins. "The very name of Gwyntystorm", MacDonald relates, "has passed for ever from the lips of men."

This is catastrophe beyond that of the drowned city in Breton and in Russian legends, for in those the city endures under the waves, unchanged, entranced, with the sound of church bells rising, at times, to men's hearing. Here there is final ruin and disintegration, or, using C. S. Lewis's word, "dis-creation", such as Lewis depicts in *The Last Battle*, in which evil is finally destroyed and the world brought to an end. But beyond that destruction lies Paradise and bliss beyond telling, whereas in MacDonald's myth the sentence of doom ends all. There is no sequel. The destruction remains an enigma. The Queen has vanished. What had happened in the mind of the author?

It has been suggested by Robert Wolff that the emotion behind the story was despair and helpless anger, that MacDonald was, at the time, overwhelmed by private grief and by general anguish for the sins and suffering of mankind. This, Wolff claims, overcame the artist in him, blurring his vision and clouding his imagination. He could no longer see the great lamp shining from the tower or find the door that would open with his golden key into the world of light.

MacDonald was indeed grievously burdened. Although intensely happy in his marriage and in the love of his children, he suffered many a loss. There was a sad hereditary delicacy in his family and some of the children died from tuberculosis. More and more, too, MacDonald became aware of the misery of the poor and of the degradation of humanity. When he wrote *At the Back of the North Wind* and *The Princess and the Goblin* his faith was strong, his imagination in control. He could say with Julian of Norwich, "All shall be well, all manner of things shall be well." Then the dark night which awaits most mystics engulfed him. The poet, the maker, the seer in him were all, for a time, overcome by anguish; only the preacher could find utterance, or the prophet who denounced evil.

Even while the darkness lasted, however, the supreme virtue of charity never failed in him. Faith, too, endured. But hope, for a while, left him, and this virtue is essential in the creative artist. His was a Franciscan soul, but at this crisis it is difficult to find in him the Franciscan spirit of joy. The darkness passed, however, and the joy recurs in his last great fantasy, *Lilith*.

Like *Phantastes*, it begins in a house: in this instance, in a library. The narrator, Vane, encounters a librarian, Mr Raven, who lived long ago. He sometimes appears in the form of a bird and leads Vane beyond the walls of the house into faerie, or into the world of Adam and Eve newly banished from Eden. Lilith, in ancient legend, was Adam's wife before Eve was created to be his helpmate. She was a witch, powerful and malignant. And this is, in the true sense, an awe-ful book. There is a vision of death as absolute dissolution, as "an invisible darkness . . . a horrible nothingness, a negation positive. . . For one ghastly moment", says Vane, "I seemed alone with death absolute."

There is nothing like this again in literary fantasy until we come to Lewis and to *The Last Battle*, with its final catastrophe or "dis-creation", followed by the "eucatastrophe" of the joyful journey to Aslan's country, to Heaven and eternity. *Lilith*, too, ends in "eucatastrophe". And, before that, interwoven in the awe-ful narrative of fall and redemption, of evil almost triumphant, there is loveliness, gaiety and innocence.

Early in his journey, Vane comes to a region where everything is tiny and delicate and exquisite. Apples are as small as cherries and of delectable sweetness. The inhabitants, the Little Ones, are innocent: they have not fallen. They are free from cruelty, malice and greed. Greed does, in fact, attack one of them, but he then grows like the stupid giants who are their foes. Vane ought to have stayed to protect the Little Ones, but he errs and neglects this duty. His way leads him on much further. He meets Adam and Eve and their daughter, Mara, the Lady of Sorrows. She is not evil, but she is tragic and spell-bound. In the end she is set free.

The landscape here is northern. It is bleak moorland, rocky and bare, looking "as if it had never been warm, and the wind blew strangely cold as if from some region where it was always night." Vane's guide is the Raven who was once the librarian and who retains human speech. He gives counsel and deals austerely with Vane's bewilderment. "Had I wandered into a region where both the material and psychical relations of our world had ceased to hold?" wonders Vane. The Raven tells him he has come through an unnoticed door into this strange region. "All the doors you have yet seen," says the Raven," and you haven't seen many, were doors in; here you came upon a door out. The strange thing to you . . . will be that the more doors you go out of the further you get in." It is Celtic, this sense of coming and going, with a door opening out of this world into another and a door leading home again.

The Raven becomes a man once more, and further instructs Vane: "You have, I fear, got into this region too soon, but none the less you must get to be at home in it; for home, as you may or may not know, is the only place where you can go out and in . . . the one place, if you do but find it, where you may go out and in both, is home." That sentence should be held in mind when we read C. S. Lewis and the adventures of the children called by Aslan in and out of Narnia.

In contrast, there is the exquisite realm of the children in *Lilith*. One of the Little People is Lona, who becomes the mother figure in this fantasy, although there is also the motherly strength of Mara, the Lady of Sorrows, in her feeling for Lilith the lost, who yet has the saving desire to be found and brought to life. Lilith, in the end, dies to live. Mara opens the door to morning and spring, wind and gentle rain, "the soft rain that heals the mown, the many-wounded grass, soothing it with the sweetness of all music, the hush that lives between music and silence. . . The sands of Lilith's heart heard it and drank it in." This is the world of new creation and the lost garden of Eden.

Vane's is the journey through Purgatory to earthly paradise, and at the end there is a vision of heavenly Paradise itself, the joyful, rushing procession which we are to find again in Lewis, after the Last Battle, when the children, their parents and all the good creatures of Narnia advance together like the redeemed in Dante's *Paradise*.

Vane finds himself among "all kinds of creatures, horses and elephants, lions and dogs—oh, such beasts. Great birds whose wings gleamed singly every colour gathered in sunset or rainbow", little birds whose feathers sparkled like jewels, butterflies and "lithe-volumed creeping things—all in one heavenly flash". Among the horse she sees the white mare he had as a child. "I needn't have been so sorry about her death," he thinks. "I should just have waited."

Here again is a stair up to the heavenly city. The children in the procession rush on, "taking heaven by surprise", and are scooped up by angelic nurses and carried off to the paradisal nurseries. The birds and beasts go to their celestial woods and to the stables of the King.

Vane is welcomed by Michael the Archangel, the standard-bearer whose aid is invoked in the Office for the Dead. He knows then that all he had ever wanted, whether he realised it or not, is coming.

On awakening from this vision, he goes through a door into his own library. It has been a true vision, sent from God. He can now await its fulfilment in peace and expectancy, living with memories, not dreams. One day, he knows, he will awaken again "into that life which, as a mother carries her child, carries this life in its bosom. I shall know that I wake, and doubt no more."

Although elements of fairy-tale remain in *Lilith*, it goes far beyond this. *Phantastes* held the promise of them but MacDonald's pure fairy tales are like the rainbow Mossy saw in the forest. At the end of his quest he climbed within the rainbow, up the stairs to the land whence the shadows fall. *Lilith* may be seen to begin where these lovely stairs end.

Chapter 4

THE SCOTTISH HERITAGE

MacDonald's awareness of an inner world, of time within or beyond our time, was part of his inheritance. It was a racial awareness, a knowledge that lay deeper than conscious learning. Behind him extended the region of legends, some from the Highlands, some from the Borders, with their memory of another race, the Little People, the conquered who had lived in the land long before the Romans or any men of history, and who, it was believed, had taken refuge in the hills, had become the hidden folk, the Good People, akin to fairies and elves, to be spoken of with respect, to be propitiated, and best left alone.

In the Mediterranean countries there was a like remembrance of the old gods, the divinities of field and wood and stream, the guardians of the hearth, long banished but not destroyed by the Christian faith. Of banished and conquered people it is prudent, as well as decent, to speak courteously.

These hidden and hiding creatures could, like the goblins, be malignant, hating the light and lurking in caves or beneath the foundations of a house. Those who care for sermons may see them as the embodiment of the evil passions which underlie the human personality. In Scottish tradition they are, for the most part, alien but not evil. They have their own laws and ways, are suspicious of human interference and curiosity, and are always on the defensive. Left to themselves, they may be harmless, but they are not without their own curiosity about humans. According to one tradition, they will not enter a house unless invited, but once invited they are reluctant to depart, and this can be embarrassing to their hosts.

Some demand human servants or victims, in some cases for sacrifice. Here is real evil, strong and perilous magic. Thus arises the unending contest between fairy and mortal: after the capture of a child or a bride or a lover ensues the long quest and the rescue. This goes back to the tales of Greece—to Alcestis, dying for her husband but restored to life; to Orpheus, seeking his Eurydice and leading her out, only to lose her again. There is a Scottish version of the Orpheus legend which tells of King Orfeo, the harper, who, when his queen, Heurodis, is taken by the fairies, follows her, and by his music so delights the Fairy King that Heurodis is set free. The ending is happy. Orfeo brings his bride safely home to his kingdom which, in his absence, has been ruled by a faithful steward.

This is one of many legends which has as its theme "the *aventures* of men in the Perilous Realm or upon its shadowy borders", in J. R. R. Tolkien's words. Three of the most famous of these legends occur in the poetry of the Borders: that of Thomas the Rhymer, that of Tam Lin and that of Kilmeny, whose sojourn in that realm MacDonald compares with Diamond's visit to the place of quietness.

Thomas the Rhymer at first mistakes the Queen of the Fairies on her white horse for the Queen of Heaven. She disowns the title, however. She tells him she has come to visit him, and compels him to ride with her on the road which is neither the broad and popular way to Hell, nor the narrow path to Heaven. It is the way after which "but few enquire". It is the road to Elfhame, and it leads through desolate country and over a river where

> They waded through red blude to the knee,
> For a' the blude that's shed on earth
> Rins through the streams o' that countrie.

Thomas must serve the Queen of the Fairies for seven years, and serve in silence. If he utters one word he will be in thrall for ever. His fee is an apple which will endow him with "the tongue that will never lee", a gift which Thomas, a realist, does not value. It will spoil his dealings at market, his gossip with the neighbours and, above all, his talk with the ladies. For how can a man drive a bargain, tell a good story or pay compliments if he has a tongue that cannot lie? To this objection the Queen pays no attention.

When the seven years have passed, Thomas returns to his tower at Ercildoune, but he is strange and changed. He is no longer at home there, and, when a second summons comes, brought by a white hart and hind from the forest, he takes up his harp and goes again to Elfhame, never to return. (One kindly tradition, however, has it that he does come back and finds refuge in a monastery, where he ends his days in peace and prayer.)

For Tam Lin there is release. Fallen from his horse at the end of the hunt, he is captured by the Fairy Queen and kept in thrall for nearly seven years. At times he appears at a well to those girls who dare to visit it, and from them takes their maidenhood, usually ungrudged. To this well comes Janet, walking swiftly, her yellow hair bound about her head and her green kirtle kilted to her knee. They love each other at sight, and Janet gives Tam more than her body. A valiant lass, she promises to set him free. On Hallowe'en she comes again to the trysting place, where at the dead hour of night

> She heard the bridles ring;
> And Janet was as glad o' that
> As ony earthly thing.

As Tam had bidden her, she pulls him from his horse and holds him fast, through every loathsome form the Queen puts upon him, until she has him at last in his own true form. He has been released from a realm more evil than Elfhame, one which every seven years "maun pay a tiend to hell"—which was likely on this occasion to have been Tam.

In many legends Elfhame is a place of disillusionment. The glamour which has lured mortals there fades, leaving bleakness and desolation. The gold turns to withered leaves. MacDonald, however, reverses this interpretation of Elfhame. Curdie at first sees only a garret with straw on the floor. Next he sees a poor old woman. Only in the end, when his sight is purged and enlightened, can he see the Queen as she really is, robed and crowned, beautiful and royal in her lamp-lit room and know her to be, if not Our Lady, then at least one of those who are near her in Paradise.

In the Ettrick Shepherd's poem, *Kilmeny*, there is neither luring nor disillusionment. For Kilmeny the compulsion is of holiness. The land where she lingers is a paradise, not the perilous realm. When, "late, late in a gloamin' when all was still", she returns to this earth, she is cherished and asked:

> "Kilmeny, Kilmeny, where have you been? . .
> Where gat you that joup* o' the lily sheen?
> That bonny snood o' the birk sae green?
> And these roses, the fairest that ever were seen?"

* Kirtle

This *revenante* can tell very little.

> Kilmeny had been she knew not where,
> And Kilmeny had seen what she could not declare.

She had gone to

> A land of love, and a land of light,
> Withouten sun, or moon, or night . . .
> The land of vision it would seem,
> A still, an everlasting dream.

The dream was a holy vision of the lost Paradise which all men seek. Bound by a holy spell, she has brought back with her paradisal peace:

> As still was her look, and as still was her e'e
> As the stillness that lay on the emerant* lea,
> Or the mist that sleeps on a waveless sea.

And she makes peace between all the living creatures around her:

> The wild beasts of the forest came,
> Broke from their bughts and faulds** the tame . . .
> And murmured and looked with anxious pain,
> For samething the mystery to explain.

The mystery, that is, of their long enmity. Now the kid roams with the wolf, the blackbird flies with the eagle. "It was like an eve in a sinless world."

Kilmeny, however, can not stay in this world. "It wasna her hame, and she couldna remain." She must return to her home in the sinless country.

> She left this world of sorrow and pain,
> And returned to the land of thought again.

Diamond also returns to the paradise of peace and expectancy.

The Ettrick Shepherd, James Hogg, was of Sir Walter Scott's generation. He outlived him by three years and was still alive when MacDonald was a boy. Hogg and MacDonald have much in common in their poetic imagination, and in their sense of holiness and magic. Also, the sense of evil which appears so vividly in *Phantastes* and *Lilith,* and only less strongly in the *Princess* books, was incomparably expressed by Hogg in that unique book, *The Confessions of a Justified Sinner,* with its inspired *diablerie.*

* Emerald
** Pens and folds

The idea of the reconciliation between all living creatures is part of the racial memory and the dream of Paradise. It is expressed in Isaiah and in the Psalms, which both Hogg and MacDonald knew well. It was part of the joyful gospel of St Francis of Assisi who saw all creation redeemed by Incarnate Love, and who welcomed Brother Sun, Sister Water and even kind Sister Death coming to receive him. "The bliss of the animals lies in this," MacDonald wrote in one of his novels, "that in their lower level they shadow the bliss of those who do not 'look before and after and pine for what is not', but live in the holy carelessness of the eternal now."

In *The Golden Key* MacDonald takes as his theme a lover's quest. It is a story of the separation of lovers and of their coming together again in the happy ending. This theme is found frequently in Celtic legend where, it may be, a girl has to find her lost lover or a king has to recover his stolen queen. It happens in *The Young King of Easaidh Ruadh,* one of J. F. Campbell's *Popular Tales of the West Highlands.* Returning from an adventure, itself perilous but successful, the King hears that his Queen has been carried away by a giant, along with his two swift horses. He sets forth to find her. At nightfall he sits down to rest and make a fire in the green wood, and to him comes the dog of the wood, a friendly creature. "He blessed the dog and the dog blessed him," telling him of his wife's plight but bidding him be of good heart and to continue his journey, but first to eat and sleep. The dog catches game which the King cooks, and they eat their supper together. Then the dog keeps watch over the sleeping King. In the morning they part, with mutual blessings once again, the dog bidding the King to call upon him in any need.

Next night the King comes to a great rock, where he rests. There comes to him a hawk, again with news of his wife in her captivity, again bringing comfort and comradeship. They sup together on three ducks and eight blackcock caught by the hawk and roasted by the King, and in the morning part with mutual blessings and the hawk's promise of aid.

On the third night the resting place is by a river, with an otter for company who is as kind and helpful as the hawk and the dog. There is salmon for supper, and, in the morning, more blessings and a promise of help.

And so the King comes at last to the place where his Queen is held captive. It is a cave, deep, deep down under a rock. The horses are there with her. The King makes his way down, and finds her. They are joyful in their reunion and together plan their escape. The giant comes back, but the Queen beguiles him into telling her where his soul, his life, is hidden. Beneath the stone on the threshold, she is told, a sheep is buried, and in its belly is a duck, and in the duck is an egg. In the egg is the giant's life.

Meanwhile the King lies hidden beside the horses, who guard him well. When the giant has gone away, the King and Queen raise the flagstone and the sheep escapes. The dog of the wood comes to pursue it and bring it back. From the sheep's belly the duck escapes, flying high in the air, but it is caught by the hawk. The egg drops into the sea, but the otter is there to dive and recover it. And so the egg is broken by the Queen, and that is the end of the giant.

On their homeward journey the King and Queen spend a night with each of the friendly creatures, feasting and rejoicing. And so, eventually, they come to the great feast in their own kingdom, after which they live happily ever after.

In another tale of seeking, *The Black Bull of Norroway*[12], there is a new dimension of sadness. It is true anguish. A girl sent out to seek her fortune is carried off by a Bull, a kind and gentle creature whom she trusts and loves. On each of the three nights of their journey they stay in a fine large house where she is most kindly welcomed. Each belongs to one of the Bull's three brothers. In each she is given a parting gift: in one an apple, in another a pear, in the third a plum, each holding jewels. These she is bidden to keep until she is in desperate need.

On the fourth day they come to a hidden glen where the Bull tells her to dismount. Here he must fight with the Devil. Both will be invisible, but, if the Bull wins, a blue light will shine; if the Devil, a red. The girl must keep perfectly still: to move hand or foot will make her invisible, and then the Bull will not be able to find her.

Obediently she sits perfectly still, hearing nothing and seeing nothing, until a blue light shines. Then, without thinking, she crosses one foot over the other. All around her there is invisibility. Long she sits waiting there, but no-one comes. The Bull cannot find her. At last she begins her despairing quest for him, herself now visible again but with none to see her.

After long wandering, she comes to the foot of a glass mountain which is so slippery that she can not put one foot after another. However, there is a smithy, and she binds herself to serve the smith for seven years, asking as fee a pair of iron, spiked shoes. At the end of seven years she is free, and, shod with iron, she climbs the glassy slope, coming at the top to a house where a washerwoman lives with her daughter. They are washing a blood-stained shirt, but however hard they scrub and rub they cannot wash the stains away. The shirt belongs to a wounded knight who has promised to marry the woman who can wash it clean. The girl knows that the knight is her lost love, the Black Bull, restored, after his victory, to his own true form. She begs leave to wash the shirt, and leaves it clean from stain. But it does not at all please the two women that she should be the bride. When the knight comes with his attendants, they assure him that the daughter has cleaned his shirt. Sadly, he agrees to marry her. The wedding is to take place on the third day.

The poor wandering girl is broken-hearted. Then she thinks of the three gifts she carries with her. The first, the apple full of jewels, she offers to the washerwoman's daughter if she may be allowed to sit by the bridegroom that night. This is granted— but the two false women give him a cup of drugged wine so that he sleeps heavily all the night through, while the poor lass sits by his bed, singing:

Seven long years I served for thee,
The glassy hill I clomb for thee,
The bloody sark I wrang for thee;
Wilt thou not wauken and turn to me?

Next day she opens the pear: the jewels in it are even finer than those in the apple. This, too, she offers for the privilege of sitting all night by the bridegroom. But again she sings her heart-broken, heart-breaking song, for again he sleeps a drugged sleep. His companions, however, do not sleep: they hear the haunting song, and, in the morning, ask him whether he had not been wakened by it. The question makes the knight wonder greatly.

That day the girl opens the plum, which holds the rarest jewels of all. Again she offers it; again she is permitted to sit by the bridegroom all night long; again the drugged wine is prepared. But this time the knight realises what is being done. He pretends to taste and to find the wine harsh, and he asks for honey to sweeten it. When the women go to fetch the honey, he pours the wine out of the window, lies down and feigns a deep slumber. His true love comes to sit by the bed and sing her song. This time he wakens and turns to her: they know each other and are glad. All that night they talk of their adventures, of their long quest for each other.

The end, as so often in fairy-tale, is swift, happy and ruthless. In the morning the knight rides off with his love and his attendants. One version of the tale says that he first kills the false women, another that he merely leaves them helpless with rage.

MacDonald's tale, *The Golden Key*, is reminiscent of this story. Tangle, too, has to journey alone for many long years before she finds Mossy again, although she has committed no fault at all and has not even been guilty of forgetfulness. But for them the bliss of the ending is beyond anything in fairy-tale.

The Black Bull of Norroway is full of ballad magic and sadness, and the song is haunting. But in some Celtic tales there is comedy. MacDonald knew all about the brownies, those helpful folk who like housework and like to reward a good housewife by doing some of her chores for her by night, and who are well pleased if a bannock, a bit of honeycomb and a cup of milk be left for them. He used this tradition in *Sir Gibbie*, where his small wandering hero for a time plays the brownie about the farms.

These homely fairies are not malicious, although they can take offence—as they do if insulted by having old clothes left out for them. They deal effectively with sluts and slatterns, which is only right. But some fairy-folk are bound by a law of their own not to enter a human habitation unless invited. Once invited, they may be very hard to evict. There is no law that compels them to go.

And this is discovered to her immediate cost but ultimate benefit by a good housewife named Imary, in an old Gaelic legend. She could not be faulted by the most critical brownie. She is capable and industrious (*eydent*, in the good Scots word)—in fact over-much so, for she will sit up late to finish her spinning or weaving long after her husband has taken himself to bed beyond the partition in the kitchen. One night, sitting at her loom, wearily trying to finish a web of cloth, she exclaims, "Oh, if only someone would come, from near or far, from land or sea, to help me!"

43

There is a knock at the door and a voice calls, "Imary, good housewife, let me in, and I'll do all in my power to help you."

Imary opens the door to a woman in green, who, without another word, sits down at the spinning wheel and begins to spin. Another knock at the door brings another woman, who takes up the distaff; then a third comes, who begins carding wool. They are welcome enough, these three, but then one knock follows another and a stream of helpers begin to fill the kitchen. It is more than Imary can bear, even though they all set to work industriously, spinning, weaving and carding the wool, and fulling and rolling the cloth. The noise they make, the birring of wheels and all the bustle and movement, sets Imary's head in a whirl. Then they all demand food. She must set the pot on the fire and make porridge, bake bannocks on the girdle and bring out her store of butter, cheese, milk and ale. A good housewife, she has a well-plenished cupboard, larder and dairy, but even so her store begins to run out. And all this while, in spite of all the activity and noise, her husband sleeps profoundly in his bed beyond the partition.

When she can bear it no longer, Imary slips out of the house and runs to take counsel from a wise man, her neighbour.

"Aren't you the foolish one, Imary, inviting the likes of Them into your house," says he, but he tells her what to do.

Back at her own house, Imary stands outside the door, crying, "Burg Hill is on fire! There is fire on Burg Hill!" Now Burg Hill is the home of the fairies. The door flies open; they come rushing out, wailing, "My children will be burned! . . . My cattle and horses will be lost! . . My meal-chest, my spinning wheel will be destroyed!"

Of Imary they take no notice at all. She runs into her house and thankfully shuts and bars the door. Then, as the wise man had bidden her, she puts everything out of action. She takes the band off the spinning-wheel, turns the loom upside down, twists her distaff the wrong way, puts the wool-cards straight and takes the pot of boiling water off the fire. With the little meal that is left she begins baking bannocks.

The Other People, finding themselves tricked, come streaming back, calling, "Let us in, good Imary, let us in."

"I cannot come to the door, I am busy baking bannocks," she replies.

"Let us in, good spinning-wheel," they call.

44

"I cannot," replies the spinning-wheel, "for my band is off, and I cannot turn."

They call to every implement but none can move. Even the pot tells them, "I'm off the fire, and the water is off the boil." They call at last to a bannock, toasting on the hearth. "I'll come," answers the wee bannock, and it jumps off the hearth and begins trundling to the door. But Imary catches it, breaks off a piece and eats it—and that is the end of the bannock. It is also the end of the invasion. In rage and frustration the Other People bang on the door, shouting and roaring loudly enough to be heard a mile and more away. And still Imary's husband sleeps on. Remembering the last words of the wise man's advice, Imary pours what is left of the water in the pot over him. He awakes, rushes to the door with a yell of rage and opens it. When the Other People see him, they know that their spells are broken, and they flee. Then all is quiet, except, perhaps, for some words spoken to Imary by her husband.

Had she lived in his time, the good cleric Robert Kirk would have added his reproof. The clergy have not always been ill-disposed to the fairies. Robert Herrick wrote of them, and that excellent Bishop, Richard Corbet, lamented their departure from England after the Reformation with, "Farewell rewards and fairies"—for they were, it would seem, "of the old profession" and loyal to the Catholic church.

The Scots cleric, Robert Kirk, wrote no poetry, but he knew the history of the fairies and knew about their supposed customs, and he recorded all this knowledge in a sober and scholarly treatise, *The Secret Commonwealth of Elves, Fauns and Fairies*. This is a unique book by a man without equal in both literary and ecclesiastical history. He was no figure of fantasy: the facts of his life are set forth in the *Fasti Ecclesiae Scoticanae* (the Annals of the Church of Scotland), that excellent compendium of parish history which is singularly free from whimsy and vain imagination.

Robert Kirk was born in the seventeenth century, the seventh child (and that is significant) of the Reverend James Kirk of Aberfoyle in Perthshire. He took his degree of Master of Arts at Edinburgh, read theology at St Andrews and, in 1664, was ordained to the ministry. Some years later he succeeded his father in the charge of Aberfoyle. He was twice married. A Celtic scholar, he produced a Gaelic psalter and had a share in the translating of the Bible into Gaelic. In 1692 he departed from this world. "The tradition is", it is recorded in the *Fasti*, "that he was walking on a 'fairy knowe' when he sank down and disappeared." Another version of the story is that he was taken up for dead. A coffin was buried in the churchyard and a tombstone was inscribed, "Robertus Kirk, A.M. Linguae Hiberniae Lumen." But did that coffin hold the mortal remains of Robert Kirk, M.A., a light of the Gaelic tongue and minister of the parish of Aberfoyle, or had he been translated to that hidden country of which he knew, perhaps, too much?

Legend has it that, after the funeral, Kirk appeared to a friend whom he charged with a message to his kinsman, Graham of Fintray, that at the christening of his posthumous son he would appear, and that if Graham, who alone would see him, would throw his knife at him, the spell would be broken and Robert Kirk would return to this world. Cold iron was said to break magic spells. The child was born; the christening was held, Robert Kirk appeared to his kinsman; but the latter was so amazed that he failed to throw the knife, and so the poor *revenant* had to go again into his place of exile, never more to be seen by man.

Kirk's *Secret Commonwealth* was left in manuscript. It reads like social history; it is as factual as any record of some little known, newly discovered country or people, full of domestic detail, as informative and as fascinating as an account by some traveller of his discovery of a remote island. It was first published more than a century after Kirk's death, in 1815.

Kirk may be regarded as among the spiritual ancestors of George MacDonald, although he did not blend magic with holiness in MacDonald's incomparable way. Neither did he, perhaps, deplore, with Bishop Corbet, the departure of the fairies. He did, however, hold that a belief in those members of the secret commonwealth was akin to religious faith, a preventive of scepticism. It is better to believe too much than too little. Respect for elves, fauns and fairies could be a form of piety. He wrote his treatise in order "to suppress the impudent and growing atheism of this age" and "to satisfy the desire of some choice friends"—to whom we must forever be grateful.

"These sithe or Fairies . . . or the Good People", Kirk tells us, "are said to be of a middle nature between men and angels . . . of intelligent spirits and light, changeable bodies . . . so pliable through the subtlety of the spirits that agitate them, that they can make them appear or disappear at pleasure." They eat and drink, feeding upon the substance of corn, drinking "some fine spiritual liquors that pierce like pure oil or air". A domestic and virtuous people, their women are skilled in all household arts, baking their own bread and weaving and embroidering their clothes which, to human eyes, appear to be of gossamer or cobweb. They follow the fashion of the country and period within which they live. In Scotland they wear the plaid.

Some of them like to visit human habitations by night, to work silently and help a good, tired housewife. Their own houses are "large and fair" but usually "unperceivable by vulgar eyes". Domestic yet vagrant, they do not choose to dwell long in one place, changing their abodes every quarter of the year. At such times they do not care to be seen of men and may punish any impertinent observer: it is discreet, therefore, to remain indoors. Some folk, adds Kirk, like a true cleric taking the chance to point a moral and show himself not likely to be fooled, attend church at such times though at few others, hoping thereby to win Divine protection against chancy encounters.

The Good People, on the whole, are harmless if left to themselves. There is one exception, which comes from that very virtue of their domesticity. Devoted to their children, they like to have a human nurse for them, and so may abduct a healthy young woman—with no thought of evil, only a lack of consideration for her own family.

In the 1893 edition of Kirk's *Secret Commonwealth* appeared a tribute to him by Andrew Lang, who was himself learned in fairy lore:

> People of Peace—a peaceful man,
> Well worthy of your love was he . . .
> Now, far from heaven and safe from hell,
> Unknown of earth, he wanders free.

Whether he is thus "far from heaven" is a fine theological point. Many would plead for his admission. Lang conferred upon him the title of "Chaplain to the Fairy Queen", which is pleasant although savouring a little of whimsy. It is tempting to indulge in that weakness and to discover a Robert Kirk, *revenant,* in our own century, in the person of that embodiment of Celtic tradition, story and song, the late Reverend Kenneth McLeod, minister of Gigha in the Hebrides. He, too, was expert in the customs of the People of Peace, and he once declared solemnly and with conviction that they liked not cake and such kickshaws, but venison.

Chapter 5

GEORGE MACDONALD AND HANS CHRISTIAN ANDERSEN

The Scottish heritage is part of the northern magic which MacDonald shared with his contemporary (his senior by nineteen years), Hans Christian Andersen. The Danish story-teller also inherited a profusion of legend and folklore, and he too enhanced and recreated all he borrowed from the past. He was introduced to British readers in the small collection of his tales translated by Mary Howitt in 1853, five years before MacDonald published *Phantastes*. This, like many later translations, may not have captured the rare qualities of his style, his homeliness and pungency, but from that moment Hans Andersen opened magic casements for British children.

The affinity between MacDonald and Andersen is not absolute. There is nothing in MacDonald to match Andersen's irony, his subtle mockery. Neither is there in MacDonald the magicking of *things*—a shirt collar, a garter, a tin soldier. Both men do, however, come very close in their awareness of the inner life and spirit of all natural things, especially of trees and flowers, and of the sun, the moon and stars. It is an awareness that goes back to Mediterranean as well as to northern myth, to Hebrew as well as to classical poetry. In MacDonald this extra sense is most alert in the perception of trees, either good or evil: the menacing Ash, the maternal Elderberry, the noble old Oak, the sad and lovely Beech. Andersen would have been at home in the forest at the foot of the rainbow with Tangle and Mossy, or in that haunted wood which Anados enters on his long journey into faery.

In their love of children, Andersen and MacDonald are of one heart. Both were aware of the evil that can threaten children, and to balance this they knew the force of pure goodness, of protective love.

The two enchanters could be realistic. Both had known poverty, although in different degrees. That of Andersen's childhood came very near squalor. In MacDonald's home it was a frugality touched with dignity, which was never insecure. There was a Franciscan quality about it which heightened his zest, his delight in the sense and savour and aspect of country things. Both men re-created their memory of boyhood.

One of Andersen's most poignant stories is almost undiluted memory. As a child he heard some censorious women scolding a boy for carrying drink to his mother, a poor, drunken washerwoman. Andersen's own mother defended her with compassion. Hence came the story *She was No Good*. MacDonald begins his *Sir Gibbie* with an account of a little dumb waif in the slums of Aberdeen waiting for his helpless drunkard of a father to emerge from the pub, then taking him home to their garret and protecting him with pure and unadulterated love.

A close kinship between Andersen and MacDonald appears in the theme of the shadow, found in Andersen's haunting and frightening tale of the shadow which gains substance and, in the end, destroys its human master (his recent translator, Erik Haugaard[13], calls it "Kafkaesque"), and in MacDonald's *Phantastes*.

In the cottage of the wise woman where Anados spends the first night of his journey, he sees, across the window, a shadow of the "large, distorted hand" of the evil Ash tree. Deeper in the forest he comes to the cottage of another woman, strange and unbenign, who yet warns him against opening a door in the back wall of the house. Anados does, of course, open the door, and he sees what looks like an ordinary broom cupboard with, beyond it, a glimmer of light. The cupboard is open, at the back, to the forest.

Then, recalls Anados, "a dark figure sped into and along the passage. . . It seemed to come within the sphere of myself, rushed up to me and passed me . . a dark human figure. . . . Its motion was entirely noiseless with ghostly feet."

Turning, he sees a dark shape lying on the floor. "It is your shadow that has found you," the woman tells him, and her face is now that of an ogress.

The shadow in Andersen's story first imitated, then dominated, then destroyed its human master. That of Anados follows him to the end of his journey. When he lies down to sleep in the wood, the weight of his body crushes the flowers, but when he rises again they revive and spring erect. The ground where his weightless shadow has lain, however, is left scorched, with every flower and blade of grass withered and dead. The culmination of horror and self-hatred is when Anados finds that, in spite of his fear, he is beginning to take a perverse pleasure in the companionship. "I need him to disenchant the things around me," he says of the shadow.

The end of *Phantastes* is the death and resurrection of Anados in that other world, his purgation and his return to his own time and place. There is a moment of anguish when he sees his shadow again, but almost at once he realises, with relief and joy, that this is only "the natural shadow that goes with every man who walks in the sun".

The treatment of the shadow theme in these stories is far beyond the scope of fairy-tales for children, but ideas are expressed which are at the root of both writers' genius.

Erik Haugaard calls Andersen "the last great teller of fairy-tales", more, much more, than a collector or reteller of folklore like the Brothers Grimm. That second claim is true, but the first assertion may be denied. MacDonald is his true kinsman and successor, fellow-heir to the riches of northern magic.

Chapter 6

VICTORIAN DOMESTIC MAGIC

Some Contemporaries of George MacDonald

The Victorians loved the idea of domestic magic. There was a dim folk memory of the homely spells of brownies and hobgoblins of the friendlier sort, those who visit and guard the hearth and who are descendants of the old gods who watched over pious families. The age of reason had dismissed them; the Church had strongly disapproved: but the canny creatures had only gone into hiding for a time and were ready to reappear.

Another element in the renewed sense of wonder was the interesting idea that *things* could come to life, that the work of a man's hands shared some quality of his personality. There were *things* in abundance in most Victorian homes, ready to be suffused with magic. The Victorian love of possessions was not entirely acquisitive: it had the grace of affection about it. The house itself was usually large with many doors, so the scene was set.

One of the most delightful of Victorian writers for children was Juliana Horatia Ewing. She wrote chiefly of domestic life and adventures, but sometimes these stories are touched by magic. She also wrote a volume of *Old Fashioned Fairy Tales*[14] and an excellent story, *The Land of Lost Toys*[15], in which toys come to life by magic. In this story, a grown-up returns, in a dream, to the place where her old dolls and other toys dwell. They have come to life and some of them put her on trial and condemn her for her neglect of them in her childhood, sentencing her to similar neglect until her favourite doll rescues her.

In her preface to *Old-Fashioned Fairy Tales*, Mrs Ewing declares that such stories can "convey knowledge of the world, shrewd lessons of virtue and vice, of common sense and sense of humour . . . of pleasure and pain." And what was even better was that they treated of a world beyond the nursery, of forces visible and invisible, of life and death and immortality. This was a sound apology, a valid defence of fairy-tales.

Mrs Ewing and her contemporary, Mrs Molesworth, who long outlived her, might be called the fairy godmothers of Victorian literature. Like all good fairy godmothers, they had an eye to the morals and manners of their children, but they were never harsh or obtrusive in their admonition, using morality rather as salt and spice to balance the sweetness of fantasy. Mrs Molesworth's particular charm is the way in which she breathes life into inanimate objects—into a piece of furniture, or a tapestry, or a cuckoo clock. In her tales, the way into faery begins in a familiar room. There is neither terror nor strangeness, but there is more than mere prettiness. Along with the charm and glamour goes a certain wholesome astringency. The children in the adventures must accept discipline as they do in their nursery. There is always a guide.

In *The Cuckoo Clock*[16] (1877) Griselda has come to stay with two old great-aunts, Grizzel and Tabitha, in their very old house which is full of treasures and heirlooms. It was "Such a house as you could hardly find nowadays. . . Time seemed to stand still in and all about the house."

Griselda is at first rebellious: everyone is so old, like the house. But the housekeeper, Dorcas, who looks after her and puts her to bed on her first night, tells her that it is a good house, loved not only by generations of its human family but also by "the good people" who used to come about it. They have not come for a long time, she says, but perhaps now, with a child in the house, they will return.

Aunt Grizzel shows Griselda the family heirlooms, including a cuckoo clock and a Chinese cabinet with mandarins and many doors. These fascinate her, especially the clock with the bird that flies out to tell the hour. But, when lessons begin, life is not all fun. The old tutor is kind, but both he and the aunts expect lessons to be carefully prepared. Griselda works in the little parlour where the cuckoo clock is. In a fit of petulance, one day, she throws a book at it, and the bird is silenced. The clock still shows the time but no cuckoo flies out of his little door. Mischief has been done, as so often in fairy-tale, by an act of wilfulness. The old ladies and Dorcas are dismayed. Such a thing has never happened before. "The luck of the house hangs on that clock," Dorcas tells the now contrite Griselda. Long ago its maker had predicted that it would bring luck, but that trouble would follow its silence. And indeed it had brought luck in the past. "There are no cows like ours," Griselda is told, "no hens like ours for laying . . . no roses like ours." Theirs has been a kind house, too, not one upset by "wrangling and jangling and harsh words", such as the Good People cannot bear. "Nothing drives them away like ill-temper or anger."

Overwhelmed with remorse, Griselda lies awake, then steals into the parlour and begs the Cuckoo's forgiveness. He flies out of his door with a clear call of "Cuckoo", scolding but forgiving her. And next day all goes happily. That second night Griselda begins her enchanted journeys, summoned and guided by the Cuckoo. He invites her into his parlour behind the clock, a cosy room rather like "a saloon railway carriage", lined with red velvet and furnished with a round table and two armchairs, with a little lamp in the ceiling like a pearl in a ring. The Cuckoo wraps Griselda in a cloak of feathers and leads her to the Chinese cabinet, which has now become a palace of many rooms with a garden beyond. Then she is led to another palace where waiting maids dress her in lovely garments: a scarlet satin skirt, a blue and silver jacket, shoes, sash, headdress and jewels. It is all done by a series of nods. The Cuckoo is always with her, protective and admonitory, curbing her impatience with, "Wait a bit and you'll see, and use your eyes. It'll do your tongue no harm to have a rest now and then."

There are other enchanting journeys. One is to the kingdom of the butterflies, where Griselda is dressed for a ball by the butterflies themselves, who cluster round her. Another is a flight, on the back of the Cuckoo, grown great and strong as an eagle, to the other side of the moon and a strange waveless sea. Griselda is taken back into the past to see her own grandmother dancing at a ball in the great saloon, with the old aunts looking not young, perhaps, but nevertheless very handsome and stately. The Cuckoo's final kindness before he leaves is to send Griselda a companion: a small boy comes to live next door. In the morning she awakens to find her pillow wet with tears. "She was happy, very happy in the thought of her kind, new friends; but there were tears too for the one she felt she had said farewell to, even though it was only a cuckoo in a clock."

In this story there is a little discipline, but no shadow of fear or danger, and in *The Tapestry Room*[17] the magic is equally

54

benign. Once again the setting is an old house, and once again a bird is the guide. The house is in Normandy—where Mrs Molesworth herself had lived for a time with her children. Her marriage had ended in a separation, made necessary by her husband's mental breakdown. From her time in Normandy came, in addition to this fantasy, a delightful book about domestic life in France.

In *The Tapestry Room*, Jeanne, an only child, is joined by her English cousin, Hugh, who has the tapestry room for his own. This, too, is a kind house, very welcoming to a lonely boy whose parents are dead and who has had a somewhat bleak existence with his grandmother. Hugh feels at home straight away. "I am sure I have seen this room before," he thinks, "I seem to know the pictures on the walls." That night a raven that had been seen walking on the terrace comes into Hugh's dream. He tells Jeanne about it next morning at breakfast by the nursery fire. The breakfast itself is delicious: crusty bread with good Normandy butter and "two great big cups of nice, hot, milky coffee . . . much nicer, Hugh thought, than the very weak tea his grandmother's maid used to give him for breakfast." Old Marcelline, Jeanne's nurse, is full of kindness.

In his dream, Hugh went into the tapestry and the world beyond it and found Jeanne there, although she herself has no recollection of this encounter. Dudu the Raven was their guide. They were driven in a coach by Houpe the cock (a real cock from the farmyard), with Grignan, the tortoise from the garden, and Hugh's own guinea-pig, Nibble, in place of horses. They were driven through the forest of the rainbows, then walked up a little stair which led to a door. The door opened upon a river bright with a light neither of sun nor moon. There they found a boat and rowed down river to Frogland, where the frogs were magic and friendly creatures. A swan sang to them "of beautiful things and sad things" and, at the end, "all grew together into one magnificent song of bliss and triumph . . . too pure and perfect to be imagined but in a dream."

This is very close to MacDonald's vision. Hugh remembers it clearly, Jeanne very dimly. Has Hugh drawn her into his dream? Old Marcelline knows all about such things. On their next journey, Jeanne is truly aware of all the wonders. Dudu leads them into the tapestry palace and up a stair to a little room where a lady sits at her spinning-wheel—a beautiful lady, white-haired and dressed all in white. She is attended by cats. The lady tells them the story of *The Brown Bull of Norroway* (a longer, more intricate form of *The Black Bull* legend). When it is finished, Hugh and Jeanne find themselves listening not to the lady in the dream, but to Marcelline, in her white cap and apron, sitting by the nursery fire with her knitting in her hands.

The children's last journey is with Dudu alone. He takes them up to the roof of the house where, under the stars, he tells them his own story and that of their great-grandmother and her sister, who were kind, in their childhood, to Charlotte, a lonely little English girl who lived near them. Years later, when they were all grown up, Charlotte and her husband rescued their French friends from the Revolution. Marcelline, the children find, knows this bit of family history.

Next morning, Jeanne's father says sadly that Dudu the raven has gone. How long he has been about the house no-one can say: Papa's father knew him. Jeanne and Hugh were prepared for this news: Dudu had said good-bye to them and told them he did not wish to stay longer.

Mrs Molesworth tells of wind and water magic too. In *The Children of the Castle*[18], two little girls pass out of time into a new dimension in the land beneath the waves. There is a reminder here of the old Celtic magic. In *Four Winds Farm*[19], the boy Gratian has an affinity with Diamond, although his adventures with the winds which blow about the farm are less wonderful and less mystical than those of Diamond with the North Wind. And he is a sturdy boy, truly of this earth. The end of the story is one of human, boyish happiness and of new friendship. The magic in this tale is very gentle, as is that in *The Children of the Castle*.

Even though he has spiritual kindred and successors, George MacDonald stands, after all, apart. To read him is almost like discovering a fairy-tale written by one of the medieval saints and mystics.

MacDonald was a friend of the Pre-Raphaelites, of Burne-Jones and Morris. One of the younger adherents of the Brotherhood, William de Morgan, craftsman, potter and latterly novelist, and a most endearing person, had a sister, Mary, who was a born story-teller. She was much loved by Morris's daughters and by the Burne-Jones children—by the next generation, also, for Margaret Burne-Jones's children,

Angela, Clare and Denis Mackail, heard the tales their mother had loved and were equally entranced. They called the story-teller "Mrs Oakchest" because she told them that her stories had come to her in an oak chest from fairyland.

These stories were published in three volumes: *On a Pincushion* (1877), *The Necklace of Princess Fiorimonde* (1880) and *The Wind Fairies* (1900). Mary's brother William illustrated the first. Most of the stories are traditional fairy-tales, but flavoured with the author's distinctive talent and personality. *On a Pincushion* has the period touch, a favourite device in Victorian tales. Each pin or brooch on the cushion tells its history.

Another story in this volume, *Through the Fire*[20], presents true domestic magic in a contemporary setting. It is about a boy, Jack (who would not be out of place in the MacDonald world of enchantment), who goes on a quest after accepting the discipline of fire. Jack is a poor boy, and a cripple, who is often left alone because his widowed mother must go out to work. One day a fire fairy appears, bidding him enter the kingdom of flame. He obeys, holding the fairy's hand, which hurts and burns but does not destroy him. Within the fire is a wonderful realm of "red-glowing hills with flames like trees and a black mountain of smoking coal". Jack comes to the King's palace of red-hot iron gleaming with flame-jewels. In the garden, among flowers which are fireworks, he meets the Princess, lovely in her flame-coloured gown, with fire-flowers in her hair, but sad because her father will not allow her to marry Prince Fluvius. However, the King's objection to a rain prince is not, after all, unreasonable.

Jack is then taken home, unscathed, but he cannot forget the sad Princess, so that when she herself comes to him on New Year's Eve, begging him to help her and the Prince, he undertakes the quest. It leads him, guarded by a wind fairy, over a moonlit sea, past the sirens with their luring song, to the far northern sea where live the seals, and men and women who are almost transparent, with ice-cold bodies and glittering eyes. This is lovely northern magic. They go on, at last, to the North Pole, and to the old man who dwells there and who will answer just one question. Jack asks, on behalf of the Princess, what she and Prince Fluvius should do.

"What puts out fire but water?" retorts the old man. "And

what dries up water but fire? . . Go back to Prince Fluvius and tell him to give her a kiss." When Jack returns he finds the Prince and Princess and gives them the message. A kiss, the Prince thinks, will destroy them both, but better to die together than live without each other. The Princess is more hopeful and wiser, saying, "We must both be changed before we can be happy."

They rush into each other's arms and are transformed. The Princess, no longer flame-bright, is lovelier than before, crowned with real flowers, and the Prince has no longer the cold gleam of water. The room is filled with a throng of fairies, all looking most kindly upon Jack. Then they vanish, leaving him alone in his poor little room.

A year passes, and the following New Year's Eve Jack is very ill. His mother, exhausted by nursing him, has fallen asleep. As he lies looking at the moonlight, the Prince and Princess come to him, bearing a gift: a magic-belt which he will neither see nor feel, but which will make him well and strong. This is their farewell. Next morning Jack awakens feeling marvellously recovered. He is no longer even crippled, but grows tall and strong and straight. None can explain his new vigour, but it is this, his mother thinks, which has cured his lameness. Only Jack knows the truth. He knows that, "It all came of my going to the North Pole for the Fire Princess."

This is a fine tale which pleased two generations of Victorian children as they sat toasting muffins by Mary de Morgan's (or Mrs Oakchest's) fire.

Chapter 7

AN EDWARDIAN SUCCESSOR

E. Nesbit

At the beginning of the new century, the theme and tradition of domestic magic were taken up by a new teller of tales whose talent at times touched genius. Edith Nesbit (1858-1924) was a born story-teller. Her first book for children, *The Treasure Seekers* (1899), and its two sequels, *The Wouldbegoods* and *The New Treasure Seekers*, contained no magic at all, but were realistic and entertaining family chronicles narrated by Oswald Bastable, the eldest boy in the family. The author was good at presenting families, and this particular quality is apparent also in the tales of magic which followed, all of which were first published as serials in *The Strand Magazine*.

In 1902 came the first of a trilogy, *The Psammead* or *Five Children and It*[21], about four London children, Cyril, Anthea, Robert and Jane, and their baby brother, known as the Lamb. While on holiday in Kent, they unearth a Psammead or sand fairy from his long sleep. Reluctantly, and with a grim sense of humour, the Psammead obeys fairy law and rewards his awakeners with a new wish every day. Having no more sense than most children, the four find this gift embarrassing rather than enriching. "Ask what you want and take the consequences" appears to be the rule. Their wish for wealth is fulfilled, but in old-fashioned spade guineas which cannot be used. That for beauty grants a beauty too dazzling for comfort. One wish does bring delight: the wish for wings. The Psammead's and the author's sardonic sense of humour is most in evidence when, without thinking, the children on two separate days make wishes about their small brother—first that he were grown up, next that everyone who saw him would want to have him. The Lamb as a baby has been tiresome. As a grown-up young man he comes very near to being, in Edwardian language, a bounder, and certainly a bore. When he is wanted by everyone who sees him, he is kidnapped, rescued, then taken again by gypsies who quarrel as to which of them shall have him. Mercifully the Psammead has conceded two safeguards to the children, one being that the servants will not be aware of the magic, the other that every spell will end at sunset. This rescues them from many an uncomfortable plight. This sort of wry humour tinged with cynicism had not, before E. Nesbit, appeared in fairy-tales. Direct retribution had always followed disobedience, but this was a new twist.

In the sequel, *The Phoenix and the Carpet*[22], the children are at home, in a dull London house in Camden Town. Their parents are moderately well off (we are told later that their father is a journalist) and, like most middle-class Edwardian families, they can afford to keep servants—a cook and a housemaid at least. But there is no splendour. Their mother buys a second-hand carpet for the basement nursery and out of its folds rolls an egg which hatches a beautiful golden bird—the Phoenix. The carpet proves to be a magic wishing carpet, ready to take the children anywhere they desire—to India or to a Pacific island, with the Phoenix as guardian. This is a lighter and happier tale than the first, full of wishes and enchantments. The golden bird has a heart of gold and all goes well. The children even do some good. They discover a lost family treasure in a ruined tower in France and restore it to its impoverished owners. Later they take a bibulous cook to a Pacific island where she is hailed as the Queen from the sea, and they similarly transport an amateur and inefficient burglar. Finally they carry off a bewildered clergyman who joins those two in holy matrimony. It is gay magic.

The third adventure, *The Amulet*[23], has a new depth and it is one of E. Nesbit's best books. The four children are left in London for what it seems is going to be a dreary summer, while their mother takes the Lamb to Madeira to recover from whooping-cough and their father goes as war correspondent to report on the Russo-Japanese war. They are staying with an old nurse in her house in Bloomsbury. Boredom is overcome when they discover the Psammead captive in a pet shop, buy him and bring him home to be hidden under a bed on a tray of sand. He is now a grateful and kinder beast, very willing to grant wishes. They find also an amulet, or at least half an amulet, which nevertheless has power. Now begin magic journeys, far backward in time and far distant in space, to ancient Egypt and to Babylon, where they are often in peril.

In their own time and place they meet "the learned gentleman", a scholar deeply versed in Egyptian and Babylonian mysteries who works in the British Museum and has rooms in their nurse's house. He becomes friendly with the children, who gradually come to realise that he has some link with the Priest, Rekh-Mara, a personage of power and menace whom they meet in the remote past. The learned gentleman is benign; the priest is a mixture of wisdom and potential evil. The two are, or should be, one harmonious personality which has been broken like the amulet. When the lost half of the amulet is found, the children have the power to bring together those divided persons, making them one. They all meet in the scholar's room. Jane, as the youngest, holds the complete amulet and speaks the word of power. "The light went out and all the sounds went out too, so that there was a silence and a darkness, both deeper and darker than any darkness or silence that you have ever dreamed or imagined." Then the light returns and with it a voice. "The light was the light no man can look upon and live, the voice was the sweetest and most terrible voice in the world." It tells the children that, although all men must live in the time and place appointed for them, a soul may sometimes reappear at a later age, in another country, and there find "a soul so akin to it as to offer it refuge . . . that thus they two may be one soul in one body." Such a refuge is given the unhappy Rekh-Mara by the benign scholar, who, in return, will receive Rekh-Mara's great heritage of knowledge. Rekh-Mara is present in the room. Jane holds up the complete amulet, now grown to a great arch, and speaks the word of power she did not know she could utter. Light shines again with "a glory and splendour and sweetness unspeakable". Priest and scholar pass under the arch and the tortured soul of Rekh-Mara is drawn into that of the gentle scholar. The light fades. The children are alone with the learned gentleman, and upon all of them has fallen a merciful forgetfulness of this great and terrible magic. The scholar is left with his mind illumined by new knowledge and understanding. For the children there is the joy of their parents' unexpected return, a comfortable, homely joy at the end of all the enchantment.

This imaginative tale seems a long way from the everyday

world of the Bastables (the family of *The Treasure Seekers* and its sequels), yet the background of both sets of children is much the same. In *The Amulet,* the domestic interludes between the magic journeys are realistically those of middle-class Edwardian Londoners. The members of both families are of ordinary intelligence and goodness, although the reader is likely to have favourites. They are not particularly heroic or noble, but they are decent, well-disposed and kind. The children of *The Amulet* show no special vocation for quests and adventures and this makes the enchantment convincing, unexpected and delightful.

And all E. Nesbit's books have, since her own day, acquired the quality or patina of period novels. Theirs is a vanished world, separated from ours by the gulf of the First World War.

E. Nesbit's last novel appeared in serial form in 1913. By this time motor cars had appeared and some of her children had the thrill of riding in one. Over the decade that separates this from her earlier novels there had been gradual changes. One, apparent in the original illustrations by H. R. Millar (which are as much part of these books as Tenniel's are of *Alice*) is in the children's dress. The four children of the *Psammead, Phoenix* and *Amulet* stories are heavily clad, the girls wearing pinafores in the house, all of them wearing long stockings and boots. In the later books, light frocks, kilted skirts, jerseys and sandshoes are all accepted wear.

Probably no writer has given such a blend of realism (appreciated now even more than at the time) and enchantment as has E. Nesbit. Her books belong to the category of social history as well as to domestic magic. This fusion of homeliness and magic appears also in two more of her books, perhaps the most endearing, *House of Arden*[24] and *Harding's Luck*[25]. (It is permitted to have favourites, and these are mine.) In these stories, children go back into their own family past, a century at a time. There is also a search for lost treasure, and the finding of the true, long lost heir.

Edred and Elfrida Arden are the last descendants of an old, noble but impoverished family. Their mother is dead. Their father has gone to South America to seek a fortune, accompanied by Uncle Jim, who is engaged to the children's Aunt Edith, and for a long time nothing has been heard of them. They have sadly been presumed dead. So, when a remote kinsman, the old Lord Arden, dies unmarried, Edred is pronounced heir.

This brings no inheritance of great wealth, but there is a considerable and delightful change of fortune. The children and Aunt Edith move from genteel poverty into comfort and dignity and go to live in the old castle on the Arden lands in Sussex. Aunt Edith is much engaged on business at first, and Edred and Elfrida are left in the care of the kind housekeeper, Mrs Honeysett. They are welcomed in the village, especially by old Beale who recognises the Arden features in Edred. They have, in fact, come home.

In the library of the castle they find a history of their family bearing the stamp of the badge of their house, a white mole. There is a rhyme too, which is to be recited "at sun-setting, by a Lord Arden between the completion of his ninth and tenth years"—which is Edred's age. At sunset he recites the rhyme to the rolling downs, and a white mole appears, addressing the children in good Sussex dialect and in forthright terms: "Don't you go for to pretend you don't know as Mouldiwarps has got tongues in dere heads same what you've got. . . All us beasts has tongues, and when we're dere we uses of them." "Dere" means in fairy-tale, and the magic has begun.

This Mouldiwarp or mole is one of the guardians of the house. (There are also two others, both larger, one being the Great Mouldiwarp of the coat-of-arms.) He comes when summoned by a rhyme, even though he thinks poorly of the rhyme composed by Elfrida. His attitude is astringent but protective.

In the attic the children find chests of old clothes. Impelled by magic to put on the clothes of a hundred years ago, they run downstairs and find themselves in the presence of a Lord and Lady Arden of a century before. They are in the England of the Napoleonic Wars, with the country under threat of invasion. And, to add further excitement, there are smugglers. Edred and Elfrida find themselves a part of these times and they are accepted by Lord and Lady Arden as their grandchildren, being subject, as a result, to severe discipline. No-one besides the children is aware of the magic, except, perhaps, an old woman in the village, reputed to be a witch, to whom Elfrida speaks gently and to whom they take gifts of tea and sugar. In one form or another, this wise woman is to reappear. The white mole is to be there too.

Meanwhile everyday life goes on very happily. The atmosphere of the old castle and the Sussex countryside, and the delight of rural life are all exquisitely conveyed. The magic recurs, always beginning in the attic with the assuming of the dress of a period in the past and always going back into a bygone century, with the Mouldiwarp as guide.

When they go into the seventeenth century, to the London of James VI and I, the children live in a great house and hear about Court life. They meet a cousin, Richard, who is presently discovered to have come, like themselves, from the twentieth century. In this adventure they fall into real danger, for Elfrida unthinkingly quotes the rhyme about Guy Fawkes. They are overheard, denounced and taken to the Tower, from which they are later rescued by an old nurse, the wise woman. On their travels they often come within sight of a mysterious hoard of treasure, without actually finding it.

Their last adventure is not through time but through distance. Helped by the moles, they go to South America and discover their father and Uncle Jim, alive but in captivity. Cousin Richard is also there, and so, too, is the Great Mole or Mouldiwarp, chief guardian of their house, a noble creature of great power. With the help of the Great Mole and Cousin Richard, who proves himself most valiant and resourceful, they all escape. At the end of the adventure, Edred and Elfrida find themselves safely at home—and soon their father and Uncle Jim return in safety though without the treasure, with a tale of having been helped to escape by a boy.

"Have I dreamed it all?" Elfrida asks herself. Past and present, magic and reality have merged. Their father is like the father they knew in King James's day, but he is their real father of everyday life, and that is such great happiness that nothing else matters. He is, of course, now recognised as Lord Arden, and he has wealth enough to put the castle into good repair and to look after the tenants, the land and the village. Life is now very good.

The sequel or companion volume to *House of Arden*, *Harding's Luck*, is the story of Cousin Richard. In this century he is Dickie Harding, a lame orphan, roughly brought up in a near-slum in Deptford by an "aunt", who is in fact no kin to him at all, but merely the owner of the lodging-house where his father died. Of his heritage he knows nothing. He cherishes, however, two heirlooms left him by his father, a baby's coral and bells, and a seal, both bearing the crest of Arden. Through these and with the help of the Mouldiwarp, who is summoned by their magic, he goes into the past and meets his cousins, Edred and Elfrida. For him, there is only one time in the past, the time of King James, where, as son and heir of one branch of the family, he is very much at home and at ease in the big house in London, or at a Deptford which is so very different from the one he knows. In the past he is not lame, but straight and strong, and, like his cousins, he remembers this modern life and its setting and tells them of life as he has suffered it: "They make people work fourteen hours a day for nine shillings a week, so that they never have enough to eat or wear. Then they put the people in prison if they take enough to keep them alive. . . Women have to go out to work instead of looking after the babies, and the little girl that's left in charge drops the baby and it's crippled for life. Oh, I know. I won't go back."

But he does. In this modern life he had met a tramp named Beale, not altogether a ne'er-do-weel, but a man of casual habits. Beale made use of Dickie in his begging when they put on an effective father-and-poor-little-motherless-son act, and he even took him on an unsuccessful burglary during which the small boy crawled through a window and opened the door. Yet Beale is far from bad at heart and he has a real affection for "the nipper". Dickie, for his part, has a sense of responsibility for Beale, something derived from his long tradition and inheritance of nobility. So, in that fine and secure Jacobean world, he remembers Beale who needs him. With the help of the wise nurse he makes the difficult journey forwards in time, taking with him some money he has been given by his father, and also his skill in wood-carving, learned from his friend the shipwright in Deptford.

Beale reforms. He remembers his boyhood in the country and his old father, and decides to go home, accompanied by a very willing Dickie. The prodigal is given a laconic but true welcome by his father, who is the old Beale we met in *House of Arden*. They settle down happily together. Edred and Elfrida's father is now back in England and comes to visit them. The children recognise each other. Old Beale has his ideas about Dickie which are shared by Lord Arden, who takes up the matter and discovers that Dickie Harding is really Richard Arden, the true heir and head of the House of Arden. Edred, Elfrida and their father belong to the junior branch of the family.

The new little lord is adopted by his kinsman, presented to the tenants as their head and generally welcomed and cherished. There is another stroke of luck for the children when they come upon a new source of magic at a stream in a cave, and find the last of the lost family treasure. All is well with the house of Arden. But Dickie will not stay. He is unhappy: he cannot bear to displace his friends. His part in his own age has been played. He feels himself exiled from his true home and age three centuries earlier in King James's England. "I can't stay here. . . I could never be happy here," he tells his cousins. And so the Mouldiwarp comes to Dickie's aid—for all three of the creatures, the small, the greater and the greatest, love him dearly. Dickie works the final magic that will take him back in time, and the Mouldiwarp will give Edred and Elfrida the release of forgetfulness. Dickie goes back: to everyone it appears that he has been drowned in the deep stream from which his body is never recovered. Edred and Elfrida grieve gently for him. They do not forget their dear cousin, but they forget the magic. As for Dickie, he is happy in his old home. Tall and strong he walks with the wise old nurse who knows and understands everything.

"All life is a dream," she had told him when he resolved to return for a while to the present, to help Beale enter his dream. Now that that task is accomplished, she bids him forget all his dreams, all the enchantment. He must now "play the man to the glory of God and the House of Arden" and dream only of the life to come, "compared to which all lives on earth are only dreams". In that life, all who have loved each other at any time or in any place in this worldly life will come together in "something more than dreams".

Harding's Luck is a complete story on its own, even though it follows and supplements *House of Arden*. Here, as in *The Amulet*, is a new dimension of poetry and mystery achieved without any loss of the Nesbit humour and realism of character and background. In *The Amulet* the magic approaches terror: there is a shadow of evil until the final good spell is uttered. In *Harding's Luck* there is a lovely gentleness, almost a touch of holiness, as there is in George MacDonald. Dickie is much tougher than Diamond in *At the Back of the North Wind,* and more comical, too, but they would have understood each other. MacDonald, one feels sure, would have loved this book.

The poetic quality in E. Nesbit recurs in *The Enchanted Castle*[26], her most complicated tale. It is rich in spells—possibly too rich. The effect is that of a Chinese cabinet full of drawers and tiny cupboards, all containing treasures, rather than of a woven tapestry which is all of a piece (as are *The Amulet* and *Harding's Luck*). It begins with mock-magic, which suddenly becomes real. Some of the adventures of the four children in the book are amusing, some a little frightening. They are, at times, caught out of their depth. In one horrid episode, figures rigged up out of sticks and brooms and old clothes come to life and are malignant. There is a mixture of beauty and terror, and returning beauty. In the castle grounds the stone beasts come alive and are overcome by splendid and serene Greek gods. They gather round a magic stone which is touched by the moon. "It is as though a spring were touched, a fountain released. Everything changes, or rather, everything is revealed. There are no more secrets. . . Space is not. . . The eternal light rests on and illuminates the eternal heart of things." The statues, come to life, hail the light. Then it fades and "softly as thistledown sleep was laid on the eyes of all but the immortals."

With sleep comes forgetfulness, merciful to mortal minds. These mortals are the four children, a French governess and the owner of the castle, Lord Yalding, who, two or three years before, had met and fallen in love with the French girl and she with him. Then, both poor, they had been separated. Now they come together again and are happy. The old theme of the discovery of treasure recurs. It is not immense treasure, but enough to put the castle in good order and let the reunited and married lovers live happily in a little splendour. At the end comes a characteristic E. Nesbit touch: she half explains what has gone before and is half sceptical. It *could* have been a dream. Yet, if it were not true, why is it that these children always spend their holidays as most welcome guests at the castle with Lord and Lady Yalding?

The Enchanted Castle, The Amulet, and *Harding's Luck* are the three peaks in E. Nesbit's work. In her later books there is still charm, excitement, realism and humour, with magic as a recurrent theme. Her talent for story-telling never flags. But sometimes the enchantment is weaker. There begins to be more than a hint of contrived magic. There is always a suggestion that it may all have a logical explanation. In *The Magic City*[27] things become enchanted; the power of the maker is expressed. The boy, Philip, builds a wonderful model city from all the things he can lay hands on in a rich house. It becomes real. The people in it come alive. Philip enters the city and, with the girl, Lucy, who helped to build it, finds himself in a new world of adventure. It is a moral tale as well as a magical one: Philip, a difficult boy, becomes reconciled with the friendly Lucy and grows amiable. This tale grew out of one of the author's own interests. She herself built a model city which was shown in a Children's Welfare Exhibition at Olympia.

E. Nesbit's last books, *Wet Magic*[28] and *The Wonderful Garden*[29], have charm. The former takes children under the sea. The latter deals with herb magic and the language of flowers. In this, the children come for the summer to the old house and lovely garden of Great Uncle Charles, which makes a strong contrast with the austere home of the ascetic though benevolent guardians with whom they have been living while their parents are in India. A runaway boy comes into the story, and again there is a moral: he has been deceitful and has to be guided into the way of truth. Again it is suggested at the end that there may have been no magic at all, and a logical solution is offered. Believe what you will.

The woman[30] who wrote these enchanting and immortal tales, showing such insight into the minds of children and such a sense of wonder salted with irony, had, herself, a happy childhood. This ended with the death of her father and two of her sisters. She became aware of the dark and precarious aspects of life. Her marriage brought further awareness. Her husband, Hubert Bland, whom she married in 1880, was a journalist (as was she herself) of versatility and brilliance, and also a man of great, too great, masculine charm. His affairs were numerous and Edith herself was by no means unresponsive to other men. As a result their household was triangular, and it was sometimes a double triangle.

Politically they were both Socialists or Fabians, and they numbered Bernard Shaw and H. G. Wells among their friends. In religion, Hubert Bland was a Catholic, although a highly irregular one in practice. Edith was received into the Catholic Church, but she was never strictly devout. She was often critical, particularly of the attitude of the Pope, as she saw it, during the First World War. But she did not entirely lapse. Her Catholicism may well have given her that sense of mystery, that *piety* in the true sense of the word, which is apparent in her best books, and her sense of the numinous which is expressed so well in *The Amulet, Harding's Luck* and *The Enchanted Castle*.

Hubert Bland died in 1914 and three years later Edith married Thomas Terry Tucker, a marine engineer and an old friend in whom she found kindliness, integrity and strength which brought her happiness which lasted until her death.

Edith Nesbit was a complex character. Her political views are sometimes expressed in her realistic portrayal of contemporary London. The poet in her loved tradition and splendour and ancient names but, above all, she loved England.

Chapter 8

THE MAGIC CONTINUES

Kipling, Masefield and de la Mare

E. Nesbit's love of tradition and of England, of the soil and countryside of Sussex in particular, which is so apparent in her two *Arden* books, links her with Kipling, whom she greatly admired. His two books of English rural magic, *Puck of Pook's Hill*[31] and *Rewards and Fairies*[32], are of the same period as the works of E. Nesbit. In Kipling's stories, too, the children, Dan and Una, go back into the past and meet Puck, who takes them deep into England's history, from Roman times onward.

Puck, like E. Nesbit's Mouldiwarp, belongs wholly to the Sussex countryside. A guardian of hearth and fields, he is one of the oldest of that Other Race who have, for the most part, left England—left, perhaps, as Bishop Corbet said in his poem, at the Reformation. Puck approves of that poem, as he does of the scenes from *A Midsummer Night's Dream*, which Dan and Una are rehearsing when he first appears. He approves, also, of the children themselves and is a kind guide and tutor. From him they learn the value of cold iron, the dignity of the oak and ash and thorn among trees, and the wisdom of the simple. Their friend, old Hobden, at the oast-house has great wisdom, and his son, the Bee Boy, whom some folk think weak in the head, knows even more. He can hold the bees in his hand without being stung, for they know him.

Puck comes often to the children. On one occasion when they are sitting in the oast-house roasting potatoes, the Bee Boy slips in, followed by Tom Shoesmith, a great fellow with a deep voice who is an old friend of the Hobdens. He talks about the "Pharisees", as the country folk call the fairies who were driven away at the Reformation. He appears to know as much as Puck about those Other People and their history. He tells the children about the Dymchurch Flitting, when the fairies all took to sea and left England. After their supper of hot potatoes, Tom

70

Shoesmith takes the children home, and they recognise in him their friend Puck.

In these tales the discovery of old England takes place through encounters with people from the past: a Roman centurion, a knight, Danes and Normans, nobles and common folk, even Queen Elizabeth herself. It is a marvellous pageant, presenting the very sight and savour of the past. It is good magic.

Something of a similar kind was done about twenty years later by John Masefield in *The Midnight Folk*[33] (1927), which was followed by *The Box of Delights*[34] (1935). Masefield's young character, Kay, discovers that his disagreeable governess, Sylvia Daisy Pouncer, is even worse than she at first appears. In fact she is a witch and the head of a coven, under the direction of a real, roaring villain, Abner Brown—a wizard so desperately wicked that we know he comes straight from fairy-tale and must, therefore, in the end be defeated and destroyed. *The Midnight Folk* is full of delightful shivers and shudders which never become real horror. There is always the reassurance of a good fairy-tale about it. Besides the people in the story, there are the beasts of the house and countryside. There is a wicked cat (the witch's familiar) and a good cat, and a friendly fox. The servants in the old house where Kay lives are kind. And, in the end, as in so many good fairy-tales, there is a fairy godmother (or someone very like one) in the person of an old friend of Kay's mother, a delightful woman who comes to take care of him and run the house. The witch and wizard are forced to disappear. And, just for good measure, there is the discovery of some very gorgeous treasure.

In *The Box of Delights,* Kay, coming home from school by train for Christmas, meets some extremely suspicious characters, who are all the more odd for being, as they tell him, members of a theological college. A travelling acquaintance of a much more admirable type is a showman who gives Kay a musical box which holds many delights. The story itself is a box of delights. We enjoy the villainy, dire plots, kidnapping and disappearances in the firm assurance that all will come well in the end. Abner Brown and Sylvia Daisy Pouncer reappear in this story. They are now married, and up to no good at all. They plot to capture the Bishop, Dean, chapter, choir and organist of the Cathedral and so prevent the Christmas service from being held.

Along with this mischief, which succeeds for a time, is the

71

narrative of Kay's discoveries in his box. He looks into a miniature forest and hears a magic song. Next, he is in the forest with animals about him. "It's all alive," he exclaims happily, "and it's full of summer!" He is looking into the very heart of summer. There is a sound as of bells, which proves to be the jingling of the silver chains worn by a great figure whom Kay first mistakes for a red deer but then perceives is a man of immense height and dignity, his head crowned with antlers. He is Herne the Hunter, who is strong and kind. He gives Kay the power to understand the speech of birds and beasts, the same gift which Mossy and Tangle were granted at the beginning of their long journey in *The Golden Key*. But Kay can also understand what the trees and flowers are thinking. Here is the old, lovely sense of kinship between all creatures, all created things. Masefield is in the direct line of descent from MacDonald.

Kay has a glimpse of timeless beauty. Then Herne the Hunter turns him into a stag and together they pace the forest. It is good, Kay finds, to have hard feet. Next he becomes a wild duck and knows the joy of flight.

The magic in the box also takes him back in time. He enters Roman Britain and meets a friendly young Roman officer who boasts of serving in "the smartest squad in the finest cohort of the star wing of the crack legion of the whole Imperial Roman army." He goes to King Arthur's court and witnesses a tourney.

In the end, after the destruction of Abner Brown and his confederates, and the release of the Bishop, Dean, chapter, choir and organist, Kay wakes up in the railway carriage where he has slept for most of his journey home from school. It has all been a dream. Professor Tolkien in his essay on fairy-tales has ruled against the dream-tale, but this is so glorious an example of it that it must be admitted among the authentic spell-binders. The reader has most willingly suspended disbelief.

In the body of both Kipling's and Masefield's work these tales of magic are, as it were, interludes, although they are characteristic of their authors. They come from a richness of imagination which amply expressed itself in this particular form, but which generally took other forms. However, in the work of Masefield's near-contemporary, Walter de la Mare, the magic is all-pervasive, enlightening his poetry and prose as well as his incomparable anthologies.

Other poets have written of fairy lore, but none have compiled such magical treasuries as de la Mare. They are suffused with enchanted light, even though most of what he selects and quotes from is long familiar. These anthologies,. beginning with the delightful and well-named *Come Hither*, are creative.

One of de la Mare's own magical poems[35], *Berries*, tells of a helpful fairy who directs old Jill, gone blackberry-picking, to the place where the bushes are most richly laden; and of Jill, having made her jelly and jam, taking a little tiny pot, an inch high, and hiding it where the fairy met her, so that the treat is shared.

But Dame Hickory, in the poem of that name, knows another kind of fairy. The voice which calls her to find sticks for her fire is that of "the False Faerie". The promise of meat for her broth pot is equally false and lures her out in vain, whereupon the dame will believe no more. There then comes the warning of a wolf, grinning and famished, at the door. Dame Hickory believes it is the fairy taking the form of a wolf. But the wolf is real. The voice now calls:

> Here's buds for your tomb,
> Bramble and lavender,
> And rosemary bloom!

and the valiant old dame retorts:

> Whsst! . . you False Faerie,
> You cry like a wolf, you do, and trouble poor me.

There is good magic—magic touched with holiness: a spell which binds together men and birds and all creatures—in *Witchcraft*[36], a good parson who looks "like a solemn, bespectacled bird". He can call all winged creatures around him to flutter and sing, not in the hope of crumbs, cheese or worms, but simply

> . . . for joy of himself and to share
> In the open of heaven his company there.

He eventually begins to think of flying away home—he can feel a sprouting on his shoulders—until one day in May he does indeed happily depart and is laid to rest. But still the birds come flocking to chirp and sing their lament, and, when night falls and all the other birds are silent, the nightingale alone sings sweetly of her grief.

73

The Other People, as Dame Hickory knew, can be evil. The story of *Miss Jemima*[37] is a perfect expression and evocation of menace. The evil is experienced by a child, Susan, who, in her old age, tells her grand-daughter about it. She relates how she stayed, unhappily, with an old great-uncle and his grim housekeeper, Miss Jemima. The old man himself was kindly disposed towards her, but helpless. Susan's mother had gone abroad to recover from an illness. In her misery and resentment, Susan took refuge in the churchyard, where, sitting on a tombstone, she saw, peering round it, a tiny face with wild green eyes, surrounded by golden hair. It was a lovely face, but it was not friendly or kind.

When she came again to the churchyard, Susan found on the stone a bunch of coral-pink berries. She ate one and heard the fairy laugh, then found her every sense quickened. The light and all the colours she could see were dazzling bright. Everything—flowers, moss, birds—"seemed as if they were showing me secrets about themselves". Mossy and Tangle had this sense of a new vision, and Kay, too, had it in the magic forest. But for them it was good magic. For Susan there was danger beneath the enchantment. She felt in harmony with the creatures about her. "I could share the very being of the butterfly that was hovering near," she recalls, "and could almost hear not only what the birds were singing but what they were saying." But the fairy's laugh was mischievous and unkind.

The face appeared again. Susan's old uncle died and, at the funeral service in the old church, Susan looked up at the east window where one of the coloured panes, broken long ago, had been replaced with clear glass. Through this looked the face of the fairy, beautiful beyond any she had ever seen, and yet evil. It was as if a shadow of darkness had fallen on the church. The face was luring her, summoning her, and the child resolved to run away. She had a vague notion that somewhere lay another country, a place of enchantment.

Early next morning she returned to the church, where the fairy once again appeared, this time at the door, luring and summoning but not daring to cross the threshold. A human footfall was heard. It was Miss Jemima, grim, hostile and angry, who scolded Susan for running away and for talking in church, and ordered her to go back. Yet, unfriendly as she was, Miss Jemima had brought deliverance. Suddenly a stone was thrown.

74

Susan was blamed and scolded more bitterly than ever, but she had not thrown the stone.

That night Susan ran away again—not to the church or the churchyard, but to the meadows where there were standing stones called the Dancers, one of which was known as the Fiddler. Again she saw the fairy—but not the fairy alone. The air seemed "full of voices and patterings and sounds of wings and instruments", a terrifying sound bringing fear beyond any she had ever felt. "The whole world seemed to turn dark and cold and dead." The child fell on the turf, fell and prayed desperately. Rising, she walked on, and saw the lights of a carriage. The night was warm; the carriage hood was down. In the carriage sat her mother, home from her voyage, well and strong and come to rescue her daughter from even more than she realised. So, the end of the story is happy. But the peril has been desperate.

There is even more potent magic, with yet darker peril, in *The Lord Fish*[38], one of the loveliest of all de la Mare's enchantments. John goes fishing and, having caught a great pike, finds inside it a golden key. Thus begins his journey into the perilous realm of the Lord Fish himself, who holds a mermaid captive. The story tells of her rescue by John, of enchantments and metamorphoses, of water-magic and of the old theme of love between a man and what at first appears to be a sea- or a river-maid, but who later turns out to be a human girl. The mermaid in this story had been transmuted by the evil Lord Fish and there is no longing in her for the world beyond the river, the palace of enchantment. It is a happy homecoming in the end to the village and John's cottage, and all the good homeliness which de la Mare conveys as memorably as he does the enchantment of the water-world.

This particular volume of tales holds every kind of magic, from the fun of *Dick and the Beanstalk* to the poignancy of *Sambo and the Snow Mountains*, where a boy "black as a bale of velvet" is made as white as snow.

In de la Mare's play, *Crossings*[39], fairies try to lure away the child, Ann. They are not so much evil as utterly strange. Sally, the kind elder sister, guards Ann, and there is a good visitor, the Candlemaker, who warns her that: "The Little People have no wasteful love for mortals," which sums up the alien nature of the fairies. Their world is not ours. The Candlemaker, whose name is Romance, is of ancient family: his ancestors, it is said, sat beneath the Tree of Life in Eden and played his bassoon. Sally is tempted to follow the Candlemaker as he wanders off into the dark, snowy woods; then she looks at Ann and instead bolts the door and stays with her. Here the magic is less explicit than in de la Mare's tales and poems.

The anthology *Come Hither*[40] is filled with magic from the moment when, as told in the preface or "story of the book", the boy Simon sets out to find a place called East Dene, of which his mother has told him, comes to the top of a hill and looks down on the old house of Thrae. Later he comes to the house and is received by the owner, Miss Taroone, who tells him about her kinsman Nahum who had loved to explore the countryside and who knew every woodland path, every stream and all the flowers and birds and other creatures. He loved, especially, to wander by night, guided by the stars.

Simon is permitted to explore the old house. "All old memories resemble a dream," and the house holds so many that it seems it might be only a shell or the "hiding-place of an abode still more enchanting."

In the attic, which had been Nahum's room, there are windows all round, and everywhere an immensity of things—a hugger-mugger of books, pots, glasses, masks and skins of birds and beasts, many strange pictures, and books beyond counting. Nahum has long since gone away, whether to return or not no-one, not even Miss Taroone, can tell.

Simon, free to explore the room, discovers two great books filled with poems which reveal Nahum's "other world" of which Miss Taroone has told him. He himself begins to see things "in a world made different or in a kind of vision or dream." And that is the story of the making of the book.

The boy falls asleep one night in the attic, awakening in the cold dawn with all the glamour gone, as happened also to those who, coming out of Elfhame, wakened on the cold hillside. There is a moment of "grief that was yet rapture" as he runs downstairs, out and away, and climbs the hill whence he had first seen the house of Thrae. He sees it again "still, wondrous, calm". He dances with excitement and then, with a wave of farewell, sets out "on the journey that has not yet come to an end".

Chapter 9

THE IRISH SUCCESSION

James Stephens and Patricia Lynch

The Other People have never left Ireland. The People of Peace, the Sidhe, the Dwellers in the Hills, in Tir n'an Og, whoever and wherever they may be, are still a part of the Irish heritage.

In the last century, Crofton Croker, in collecting some of *The Fairy Tales of Southern Ireland,* did for Celtic lore and tradition what Joseph Jacobs did for English. Both compiled treasuries for future generations.

In 1920 that entrancing creature, who seemed himself to have come out of the borderland between this world and the other if not from Elfhame itself, James Stephens, produced his *Irish Fairy Tales.* These legends of Fionn and Oisin, of gods and heroes, were retold with incomparable wit and vivacity, full of poetry and of a glamour that has no tinge of whimsy. He followed this with other retellings and recreations of the great and sometimes tragic legends of Ireland, legends of epic grandeur and haunting power such as *Deirdre*[41], and that of Midir and Etain which is the main theme of *The Land of Youth*[42].

This book begins briskly: "It was decided that the evening meal should be eaten on the lawn before the palace." The evening is the feast of Samhain, "the one night of the year in which whoever has the will and the courage may go to Faery," the feast that is now Hallowe'en. It is the eve of the joyful and holy festival of All Saints, but even with such Christian hallowing it is an awesome and uncanny time. As the company gather within the circle of fire and torchlight, Queen Maeve tells her children of the delights awaiting them—of the many kinds of broth, fish and meat, the wine from far countries and the mead made by her from the honey of her own bees.

Meanwhile Ailil the king waits in his tent. "I wonder would any man dare go abroad tonight," he muses. "I seem to hear already the brisk tread of the people of Dana moving out there beyond the light." The people of Dana are the old people, dispossessed or hidden. They are gods or fairy, as you will. They are indeed there, and soon the marvels and enchantments begin.

James Stephens was a poor Irish boy with a rich heritage of legend. In everyday life he was a solicitor's clerk in Dublin, the Dublin of Yeats and AE (George Russell). In 1912 he published *The Crock of Gold*[43], a book of pure genius and one of those unique masterpieces which it is impossible to place or define. It is unique even among the author's other and kindred books. It was reviewed by Walter de la Mare who, more than forty years later, after Stephens' death, quoted himself in the foreword to a paperback edition: "Like half the best books it is more than a little mad, and it is crammed full of life and beauty." The madness has an extraordinary lucidity. The narrative is coherent once the reader has accepted the existence of another world and the reality of its inhabitants, who may have unusual powers and knowledge but who are divertingly and convincingly human. The tale introduces two philosophers, husbands of the Grey Woman and the Thin Woman, and gives a pungent account of these marriages. Among the deities or semi-deities are Angus Og, Angus the Ever-Young, hero of Irish legend, and Pan, who may have appeared first in Greece but who is ubiquitous. The developments of plot are too complicated to summarise, but the ending is happy.

James Stephens, like Walter de la Mare, wrote much and variously, both poetry and prose. In all his work, along with frequent strong realism and irony, there is always *glamourie*.

The writer with whom he has most affinity is also Irish. Patricia Lynch, who from the 1930's on wrote spell-binding tales, provides a treasure of fairy gold which, unlike that in most legends, does not turn to withered leaves.

She was born in Cork into a large household, with her grandfather, who was a scholar, at its head and including uncles and aunts as well as Patricia's mother and brother. Her father, however, was abroad. One day a letter came from him, asking her mother to join him. It was all very well for her to take Patricia's brother with her, but Patricia herself was too young to travel so far. The aunts would gladly have kept and cherished her, but to her joy and unending profit it was arranged that she should go for a time to stay with Mrs Hennessey who lived in the country and sometimes came to

78

Cork. Now Mrs Hennessey "was a shanachie, one of the real old story-tellers" like her father before her. She knew all the old tales of the people who had lived in Ireland before history began and who were "as well known . . . as the neighbours in her village". For the child's grandfather she had the respect due to his learning—but he had too much learning in his head to have room for stories.

And out of that period in *A Storyteller's Childhood*[44] (as Patricia Lynch called her autobiography) came her birth as a writer. There was a spiritual kinship between Patricia and Mrs Hennessey. The woman awakened the child's imagination and fed her an unending diet of tales. Furthermore, she passed on to her the method of story-telling. All this took place in a setting of country life which would later form the background to many of Patricia's own stories.

Later, when Patricia's mother came home again, they lived for a time in London, where Patricia discovered the lending library with its shelves upon shelves of books, many of them full of delightful stories. Among them were those of E. Nesbit, and from one blissful exploration of the library shelves she came home with *The Magic City* under one arm and a volume of Greek legends under the other.

At her convent school Patricia was praised for her essay-writing and encouraged both by fellow pupils and by the nuns to tell and to write stories. The making of the story-teller was already complete. In her own Ireland there was an immense treasure of tales to be retold, although more often than not the mere idea or suggestion of a tale was sufficient to set her creative mind to work. The story-teller is, like the poet, a maker, and this particular story-teller created magic worlds full of real characters, whether human, fairy or animal.

In *The Turf-Cutter's Donkey*[45], Seumus and Eileen are the children of the turf-cutter who "knew so many songs to sing and so many tunes to whistle, that he hadn't a deal of time for turf-cutting." They live in a white cabin near the great bog where their mother makes and sells exquisite lace. They keep a little red Kerry cow, a fine pink pig, quantities of hens and chickens—and the donkey, rescued by the children from the tinkers. The tinkers play a vigorous part in the adventure. And there is also a leprechaun. A silver teapot is discovered which the children's mother recognises as the one stolen from her grandmother when

she herself was a child, and which is full of golden sovereigns—
no fairy gold, either, to vanish or turn to withered leaves, but
real gold, which means that they can build a bigger and better
cottage with a stable for the donkey, Long Ears. And that is only
the beginning of the story.

Seumus and Eileen go to the Fair, where the leprechaun
haunts them, demanding his share of tea and apple cake and a
ride on the roundabout. And so does the pig. A man comes from
the bog bringing gifts, and the fairy-tales in the book Eileen is
given are re-enacted. The children meet Finn. They see the
battle of the Dana against the Firbolgs. They are welcomed at a
feast where the magic cauldron provides every guest with the
food of his or her choice, and Eileen is saved from drowning by
the salmon of wisdom. Then they come back to the whitewashed
cabin with smoke curling from its chimney and think that in all
their adventures they have seen nothing lovelier. This Irish
magic is homely and enchanting, comic and convincing.

In the sequel, *The Turf-Cutter's Donkey goes Visiting*[46], the
magic continues. The story involves the captain and mate of a
barge and a somewhat disagreeable cousin. And the leprechaun
is there again. It is a funny and wholesome book, its humour
somewhat astringent. There is sometimes a reminder of
E. Nesbit, that most English of story-tellers, in this Irish
enchantress. But Patricia Lynch has her own way of
enchantment which is at once highly individual and entirely
national. Only the Irish heritage could have produced her
particular riches.

The leprechaun in these books is used as a sketch for a
finished portrait which is begun in *Brogeen Follows the Magic
Tune*[47] (1952). Many tellers of tales have told about leprechauns
but there is only one Brogeen, so full of life and strength of
character. His adventures and encounters were developed by
Patricia Lynch over some twelve years of writing. He is all the
time in and out of the Fairy Fort of Sheen, but unlike most of the
Other People he has no desire to lure humans within that
boundary. His chief desire is to come, himself, into this human
world. Brogeen loves people, but loves them without
sentimentality and with a keen critical faculty, and he enjoys
their food, their homes and their habits. A fairy feast is all very
well in its way, but much better, to his mind, is good human
food. He loves pie, sausages, eggs, apple or soda cake,

sandwiches and tea—lashings of tea, hot, strong and sweet. At the end of of his last sojourn amongst mankind, in his house at the root of the beech tree where birds and squirrels are his neighbours and Jim and Judy MacDonald and their mother are frequent visitors (bringing always a full basket), he holds a party for the King and Queen of Tir n'an Og, who stuff themselves happily and gratefully with sandwiches, sponge-cake and tea. "Why don't we have this wonderful drink in Tir n'an Og?" asks the Queen, holding her cup to be refilled.

Brogeen begins his wide human friendships with Batt Kelly, the fiddler, and in the course of his wanderings he acquires many more human friends, and one or two adversaries as well—notably the Black Enchanter. He has various animal companions, too, especially Trud the little elephant.

In these stories, and indeed in all Patricia Lynch's stories, there is a delightful sense of danger. There are plenty of plots and attacks, wizardry unlimited, enchantments, beguilings—but no real evil. There is always a fundamental sense of security. Whatever happens to Brogeen and his friends, we know that all will be well in the end. However, life would indeed be dull without adventure. In these tales there is always, as there is in all the best fairy-tales, a sense of law, fairy law. Brogeen is a privileged citizen: he can get away with more than most. But there is a limit, and he knows it. He may be a vagabond but he is not lawless, and above all he is a lover of the home. "Travelling is grand," he reflects when, in *Guests at the Beech Tree*[48], he comes back for the last time to his house in the beech wood. "But where's the sense of having a home of yer own if ye're never in it?" He reflects further: "A leprechaun that doesn't make shoes has no rights at all." If he keeps on dodging his job, he may not be allowed back into the Fort of Sheen, and so may be in exile for ever from Tir n'an Og.

So Brogeen's last adventure ends with his return home. He has made shoes for the Queen and she and the King have come to his party and been delightful and delighted guests. They depart with courteous thanks. Brogeen stands at the door of his beech-house and exclaims: "I've never seen a better party in all me born days." He goes in and shuts the door. That is the end of the tale—but we feel sure that before long he will go back to the Fairy Fort and be welcome.

Chapter 10

THROUGH THE WARDROBE

The Magic of C. S. Lewis

The enchanting idea of sending children through an old wardrobe into a new kingdom of men, animals and minor deities would have delighted E. Nesbit. It is found in the work of her admirer, C. S. Lewis, who read her not in childhood but in maturity. He continued her tradition of domestic magic. He saw the possibilities of a large house with lots of spare rooms and cupboards from which strange doors might open.

Like E. Nesbit, he contrives to keep parents, however admirable, out of the way. In *The Lion, the Witch and the Wardrobe*[49], four children, the Pevenseys, Peter, Susan, Edmund and Lucy, are sent to stay with an elderly professor in his country house. The period is the Second World War, when hosts of children were sent away from the cities to be safe from air-raids. The Professor is benevolent but remote, his housekeeper forbidding. The children are left to amuse themselves.

It is a grand house for hide-and-seek, and Lucy, in one game, runs into a spare bedroom and climbs into a great wardrobe among some fur coats. At the back of the wardrobe she finds the door which leads into Narnia and into the first of seven adventures.

"I wrote the books I should have liked to read," Lewis has said of these chronicles. "What I would have liked to read when I was a child, and what I still like to read in my fifties." This first tale is also full of wonderful things he would have liked to eat. Writing with a memory of the rationing and austerity of the war, he describes very succulent meals enjoyed in Narnia.

Lucy first goes into Narnia in the dead of a long winter and finds the kingdom in thrall to an evil witch-queen. She is greeted by Mr Tumnus the Faun who is carrying an umbrella, some parcels and his own tail over his arm to keep it out of the snow. In his warm little house he gives her tea, with eggs and sardines, buttered toast, cake and honey. The cosiness of the scene is enhanced by pictures and a bookcase containing such scholarly and enticing volumes as *The Life and Letters of Silenus, Nymphs and Their Ways* and *Is Man a Myth?* Mr Tumnus is a delightful host, which makes his sudden collapse into tears all the more alarming. He confesses, with contrition, that he has been sent by the evil Queen to capture Lucy, but he has resolved, instead, to lead her back safely to her own world.

Lewis has declared that he *saw* all this, saw the faun walking through the snow with his parcels, his umbrella and his tail over his arm, saw it as clearly as Lucy did. This picture was followed by a sequence of vivid images including, finally, that of Aslan the Lion, the glorious and strong son of the Emperor beyond the seas who has created Narnia and who will save it. He calls the children to help him with this deliverance. "I don't know where the Lion came from or why he came," Lewis recorded. "But once he was there, he pulled the whole story together, and soon he pulled the other six Narnian stories in after him."

There is about the *Narniad* (as one devoted reader has called it) a sense of compulsion, of one power or personality controlling the characters and events, both good and evil, until the end. Lewis saw the great potential of fairy-tale for expressing his ideas[50]. "I fell in love with the form itself," he recalled, "its brevity, its severe restraints, its flexible traditionalism, its inflexible hostility to all analysts." Only those ignorant of the creative process could believe that he deliberately set out to "say something about Christianity to children", using fairy-tale didactically and patronisingly. It would be more accurate to say that fairy-tale used him. Similarly, the Christian element simply "pushed itself in" without being deliberately contrived. Lewis was not merely a Christian, he was in love with Christianity. The lion Aslan compelled him, becoming more and more clearly (though never by the author's specific assertion) the type or emblem of the Redeemer, the Creative Word, the *Pantocrator*.

The literary form used here is far from easy. It has strict rules and requires as much discipline as the writing of a sonnet or a work of scholarship. Fairy-tale can sometimes be the best, even the only way of saying what has to be said. In such a story there must be both plot and theme—the two are not synonymous. Plot is necessary: a story must be told, but "the plot is really only a net whereby to catch something else. The real theme may be . . . something other than a process, and much more than a state or quality." The net must be strong enough to hold it.

There are three ways of writing for children in Lewis's conception of the craft. One is bad: that of writing down, of being coy and self-conscious, of giving children what the author thinks they should want. Two ways are good. One is telling a tale to please certain specific children, as Lewis Carroll did with *Alice in Wonderland,* and then giving it to the world. Kenneth Grahame told his small son Alastair all about Rat, Mole and Badger before he produced *The Wind in the Willows.* J. R. R. Tolkien told his own children about *The Hobbit* and received helpful criticism. The other way is writing, as Lewis did, under compulsion. Tales thus written are likely to hold adult readers as well as children.

"I am almost inclined to set it up as a canon that a children's story that is enjoyed only by children is a bad children's story," wrote Lewis. "The good ones last." His own discovery of E. Nesbit and his delight in her as an adult is an instance of this. The mature, even the scholarly mind, does not outgrow good fairy-tales but continues to enjoy them along with other classics of fiction, drama and poetry. (The reverse is also true: some adult novels have become children's favourites. When there were few if any books written directly for children, they in their wisdom annexed such masterpieces as *Robinson Crusoe, Don Quixote, The Arabian Nights* and *Gulliver's Travels.*)

As an example of plot holding theme as in a net, Lewis gives *The Hobbit.* It is in the true tradition of fairy-tale, with a strong plot full of events and danger and with characters to hold our interest and entertain us. But there is much more besides. "As the humorous homeliness of the early chapters, the sheer *Hobbitry,* dies away," wrote Lewis, "we pass insensibly into the world of epic."

He found this extra quality in *The Wind in the Willows.* This is far more than a lively account of animals in their own world, given human trappings but keeping their own nature. It is an idyll; it is comedy of character; it is social history. The characters may be animals, but they reflect humanity. The friendship between the good Rat, Mole and Badger is like true human friendship. They all show equally human exasperated patience when dealing with Toad who, although not bad at heart, has the vulgarity of wealth and is almost completely devoid of intelligence. The three friends are distinct each from the other. Rat is genial, easy, well-mannered and tactful. Mole is a little shy and ingenuous. Badger, older than the other two, is, in Lewis's words, an "amalgam of high rank, coarse manners, gruffness, shyness and goodness". He has something of the old squire about him. "The child who has once met Mr Badger", says Lewis, "has ever afterwards in his bones a knowledge of humanity and of English social history which it could not get in any other way."

Similar knowledge is to be gained from Kipling's *Puck of Pook's Hill* and *Rewards and Fairies*. Puck teaches Dan and Una the very essence of England's history. He is English and of the earth, the Sussex earth. The scene in the oast-house where the children roast their potatoes at Old Hobden's fire and listen to his talk and that of Tom Shoesmith, whom they accept as Old Hobden's friend, has the same value as the meeting with Mr Badger.

In *The Wind in the Willows* there is, as well, much goodness of heart. Badger is benevolent towards the hedgehogs who take refuge from the snow. To them he is very much the great gentleman, the old squire. Mole welcomes the field-mice on Christmas Eve, and to them he too is the kind gentleman. And with them comes the sense of the numinous as they sing their carol of the beasts:

> Who were the first to cry Nowell?
> Animals all, as it befell,
> In the stable where they did dwell.
> Joy shall be theirs in the morning.*

There is no incongruity between that Christian joy and the worship which Rat and Mole pay to Pan, their own deity, when they come to the islet and find the lost baby otter lying safely at his feet. They adore him and are glad. Pan is benign, and yet they are filled with a holy fear.

Lewis loved this book and in the first of the Narnian tales, *The Lion, the Witch and the Wardrobe*, the encounter of the four children with the good Beavers brings us close to the domestic life of Mr Badger. The children come out of the bitter cold into the warm kitchen where Mrs Beaver is preparing dinner. The potatoes are in the pot and the kettle is boiling. Mr

* Kenneth Grahame, *Wind in the Willows*, Methuen.

Beaver goes out to catch some trout and they all feast heartily, ending the meal with a large, hot, sticky marmalade pudding. There is, however, an essential difference between this scene and the one in Badger's house. Rat and Mole find shelter, warmth, food and a welcome, but it is only for the night; next morning they set off home. For the Pevenseys this is only the beginning of adventure and peril. After dinner Mr Beaver tells them of the doom lying upon Narnia, of the part they can play in its deliverance, and of Aslan. Then they find that Edmund is missing. In this first chronicle he plays the traitor, seduced by greed.

The echoes of *Wind in the Willows* die away as Lewis develops his own theme, but they have been clear and delightful. There are echoes too, of Beatrix Potter: "what I can only describe as the idea of Autumn", when reading in *Squirrel Nutkin.* "One autumn, when the nuts were ripe and the leaves on the hazel bushes were golden and green, Nutkin and Twinkleberry and all the other little squirrels came out of the wood and down to the lake."

Beatrix Potter's animals stay away from men, even though they may live in houses and wear clothes to be laundered by Mrs Tiggywinkle. Rat and Mole also, for the most part, live in their own world of river and wood. Once, on Christmas Eve, they pass through a village, see the lit windows and are aware of kindly human life. This wakens in Mole an acute nostalgia for his own *dulce domum* and leads to his return home and to a happy Christmas Eve with carols. In Narnia there is friendship between the children and the animals: all unite against the forces of evil.

Like his hero George MacDonald and his friend and contemporary J. R. R. Tolkien, Lewis was more than a teller of tales: he was a maker of myths, a scholar and a teacher. His scholarship underlies his story-telling.

There was another contemporary with some kinship of mind to Lewis and this was Charles Williams. He shares with the others what Charles Moorman (in *Arthurian Triptich*) has called "the sort of sacramental mentality" which expresses itself in myth. Charles Williams did not write fairy-tales. His kinship with Lewis is best seen in the similarity of his work to Lewis's adult fantasies, *Out of the Silent Planet, Perelandra* and *That Hideous Strength;* in his retelling of the Cupid and Psyche myth, *Till They Have Faces,* and perhaps also in the famous *Screwtape Letters,* although these have a wit and pungency absent from anything in Charles Williams.

All four authors were Christian in belief and practice. Three of them were Anglican, Tolkien was Roman Catholic. All shared the sacramental heritage. Dr Moorman has found in Lewis and Tolkien a reflection rather than a statement of the Incarnation and the Atonement, an expression of that co-inherence of all things in God which was at the heart of Charles Williams's teaching. In Lewis, the friendship between the four children and the people and creatures of Narnia is a lovely parable of this doctrine.

Looking briefly at Lewis's life and other work, we find it best explained in his autobiography, *Surprised by Joy*[51], and in various of his essays and letters. These make vivid and comprehensible his adult fantasies and his *Narniad.* He acknowledges many debts. "The greatest of these", he wrote, "I owe to my father for the inestimable benefit of a childhood passed, mostly alone, in a house full of books."* That childhood would appear somewhat austere to a modern child, but it was secure and, after the shock and grief of his mother's death, emotionally peaceful. His father was kind, again in what might seem today to be a remote way, but the Edwardian boy did not expect his father to be a playfellow, and with remoteness there can be a wholesome lack of possessiveness. Freedom with security, a large house and garden and a copious variety of books was enough to make this boy contented.

Clive Staples Lewis was born in Belfast in 1898, the second son of a lawyer. His brother and he were on excellent terms. The house had little beauty of furnishing or pictures but it had space, with corridors and attics and, everywhere, books—some on the landing in a large bookcase, some stuffed away in the attics. There was such an abundance of them that it was almost as if the books grew. Such a setting was familiar to many middle-class Edwardian children. Today it seems almost as strange as a castle or stately home.

Not many of the books in the house were intended for children. Some may have been quite unsuitable. But none was forbidden. And a child intent upon reading can enjoy and absorb almost anything.

Lewis's school life was unhappy, but after a time he was sent

* From Lewis's preface to *The Allegory of Love.*

to a tutor, W. T. Kirkpatrick, a true scholar and a true teacher who wakened the boy to the discovery of Greek and Latin as living literatures. Lewis began even to think in Greek. This was the beginning of his own scholarship, his first awareness of the European literary tradition.

There was not much poetry among his father's books, but there was one poem by Longfellow that gave Lewis that feeling of "northernness" which he was to love in other men's work and express in some of his own. (This same feeling is, of course, strong in MacDonald, in Tolkien and in William Morris.) The line which impressed Lewis was: "Baldur the beautiful is dead, is dead." The boy knew nothing of the Norse sagas, but this was enough to lift his imagination "into huge regions of northern sky".

This love did not conflict with his other love and discovery, the Mediterranean world, its culture and pieties. Above all, Lewis loved Italy and the Italian epic, deploring the modern neglect of Tasso and Ariosto, once the reading not only of scholars but also of men and women of education and culture, including well taught girls, for whom it took the place of the Latin and Greek absorbed by their brothers.

Lewis's scholarship was part of himself. It touched and fortified his imagination as well as his intellect. The discipline helped to shape his fantasies and the zest he had for story-telling is apparent in his research.

His adult fantasies, especially *Perelandra*[52], have the same relation to his Narnian chronicle as MacDonald's *Phantastes* has to his fairy-tales. Ransom, hero of Lewis's fantasies, travels beyond this world into *The Silent Planet* and there meets Meleldil, the Redeemer figure. In *Perelandra* he comes to yet another world beyond ours—a lovely world which has known no fall and which has none of our measurement of time. There he meets the Green Lady, a figure like *Primavera*, another Eve, but an innocent Eve, unflawed by disobedience or self-will. She is virginal rather than maternal. Ransom's account of earthly measurements of time fascinates her. She is interested to hear, "How a day has one appearance as it comes to you, and another when you are in it, and a third when it has gone." She is utterly bewildered by his talk of death, a thing unknown in this Eden. It is a thing so terrible, Ransom tells her, that "Maleldil himself wept when he saw it."

Then he gives his account of our world, of fallen mankind, of the sickness brought by Eve's disobedience and healed by Mary's response. The Lady sings her own Magnificat: "I am the Mother. . . My spirit praises Maleldil who comes down from deep heaven into this lowness, and will make me to be blessed by the times that are rolling towards us. It is He who is strong and who makes me strong, and fills empty worlds with good creatures." (This filling of emptiness is also shown in one of the tales of Narnia.)

The Lady, in her sinless world, is something like Kilmeny in her grace and gentleness and loveliness. But there is none of Kilmeny's longing, for this Lady has never known banishment.

Evil now enters her world in the person of Weston, the arch-enemy, already encountered by Ransom. He reminds Ransom that in the human world the *felix peccatum* had brought the Redeemer, God Incarnate. "Whatever you do, He will make good of it," Ransom tells him, "but not the good He had prepared for you if you had obeyed Him. That is lost for ever."

Weston is incarnate evil, living hatred, enmity towards God. He has a positive terror of good. He is defeated. Tor, who is the King, comes with his Queen to rule Perelandra, his kingdom. He prophesies that in the human world there will be salvation. Maleldil will send his messengers, then come Himself. At His coming there will be the annihilation of evil, the dis-creation of this marred universe. That promise is fulfilled in the last chronicle of Narnia, *The Last Battle*.

"Where Maleldil is, there is the centre. He is in every place. . . Because we are with Him, each of us is at the centre. . . He has immeasurable use for everything that is made. . . We also have need beyond measure of all that He has made." This doctrine of total redemption for all that have but a grain of goodness, the idea of coinherence, of all creation subsisting in Christ, is at the heart of Lewis's Christian belief as well as that of Charles Williams and of Tolkien. It recurs in the Narniad. It is the teaching of St Paul.

Perelandra ends with the annihilation of the arch-enemy. Then comes the great dance, like that which Dante saw in Paradise. Perelandra has become Paradise, bathed in supernatural light.

Chapter 11

NARNIA

C. S. Lewis

From Perelandra, that paradise not lost but guarded, we come to Narnia, created in primal loveliness, attacked and haunted by evil, redeemed and made the way to heaven. In these tales there is again a variety of creatures co-existing. There are the Narnian people and their animals, creatures from legend and children from our own world. All are drawn together by Aslan. There is a variety, too, of elements such as fantasy and comedy, grandeur and homeliness, valour and danger.

The old fairy-tales go deep down to the roots of tradition and race memory. They grow like trees or grass and the true story-teller is like the character in legend who can hear the grass grow. Robert Kirk spoke the truth when he declared that a belief in elves, fauns and fairies was better than no belief at all. It could lead to true faith. Faery lies on the borders of that lost Eden for which there is a racial, a human—perhaps an animal—nostalgia, hence the kinship and comradeship between men and beasts and birds, even between creatures and woods, streams and trees, and the help given by birds, fish or animals to fairy-tale heroes in return for some kindness.

Narnia is full of benevolent talking creatures, very distinctive in character one from the other. Glimfeather the owl, Reepicheep the mouse, Bree the horse, beavers, bears and dogs are all part of the community. All are threatened by the invading evil and all share the defence of Narnia. They all share in the final joy of meeting again, of recognising and being recognised, some of them after a long separation. The light of *caritas* illuminates them all. This is charity, the pure love felt for all creatures and things in life for their own sake as part of the creation of Divine Love.

Lewis, like Kenneth Grahame and Beatrix Potter, can create comic characters. His laughter is kind and loving; it is never mockery. Reepicheep the mouse is funny and heroic at the same time. The idea of total redemption does not destroy the imperfect or the absurd, only the utterly evil. A shy, imperfect worship is not despised. It is considered better to believe in those Other People, to worship Pan and the gods of wood and stream, than to hold no belief and to give no adoration at all. A saint is none the worse for being confused or allied with some pagan divinity. Pan may walk humbly and with attempted decorum behind St Francis.

Lewis has the same gift as E. Nesbit for creating ordinary children—or a little more than ordinary, perhaps, for they have a capacity for accepting magic. He also shares her gift for presenting distinctive characters. The four Pevenseys are members of one family, but each has shades of difference. Lucy, the first to be drawn into Narnia, is obviously the author's favourite. She carries the light of her name about her. She is responsive and courteous, accepting marvels and marvellous creatures with friendly calm. The others are, at first, sceptical, and, in the first tale, *The Lion, the Witch and the Wardrobe*, one of them, Edmund, is hostile. The other two, Susan and Peter, accept the reproof and assurance of the Professor, who is not at all surprised by Lucy's account of her adventure. They are thus prepared for their journey into Narnia, where they are to take part in the danger and defence and to learn to be valiant and faithful. Peter remains steadfast. Edmund is a rebel and a traitor, tempted by sheer greed, but he is converted. He knows utter contrition or *metanoia,* yields himself wholly to Aslan and is thereafter a devoted follower.

When, at that delicious dinner with the beavers, Aslan's name is first spoken, Edmund feels a strange horror. Peter feels brave and adventurous. For Susan it is "as if some delicious smell or some delightful strain of music had just floated by her". To Lucy the name brings the feeling one gets when awakening in the morning and realising it is the first day of the holidays or of summer. Presently Father Christmas arrives, bringing them "tools, not toys" to be used in times of need. For Peter there is a sword and shield, "a very serious kind of present". For Susan there are a bow and arrows, and an ivory horn. For Lucy there is a tiny bottle of a healing cordial made from "the juice of one of the fire-flowers that grow in the mountains of the sun".

So it all begins—the warfare, the enchantments, the treachery, the valour and the final redemption of Narnia by the death of

Aslan, the great golden lion. Soon after Aslan's appearance had come Edmund's contrition and his *metanoia*. Walking apart with Aslan, he had confessed to him. On the night before his death, it is Susan and Lucy who walk with Aslan, their hands on his mane so that he feels the comfort of their touch. Then he bids them leave him, and he goes alone to his agony and his death on the great stone table. At sunrise the table is found cracked from end to end. Aslan is not there. The children hear his voice, turn around and see him alive and more glorious than ever.

The long winter is over. The evil Queen and her forces have been routed; the enchantments have been lifted. The four children become kings and queens in Narnia, with Peter as the High King. All the good creatures are free and happy. The golden age has returned. How long they reign, the four cannot tell, but they remain in Narnia until, one day, hunting a white stag, they come to a part of the wood which is strange, yet dimly remembered, and find themselves making their way not through trees but through coats hanging in a wardrobe, and come tumbling out into the spare bedroom in the Professor's house where none has noticed their absence.

The Professor hears the account of their adventures without surprise. It is what he expected. They will not return to Narnia through the wardrobe, he tells them, yet one day, when Aslan calls them, they will go back. "Once a King in Narnia, always a King in Narnia," says he. "It'll happen when you're not looking for it." Meanwhile let them not talk of it, he warns, even among themselves.

They are compelled to return suddenly, yet they are unsurprised. In *Prince Caspian*[53] they are at a railway junction, waiting for the trains to take them back to their respective schools, when they suddenly find themselves in their former kingdom, "coming back to Narnia", as Peter says, "just as if we were Crusaders or Anglo-Saxons or Ancient Britons or someone coming back to modern Britain."

Many years of Narnian time have passed since their first reign. Again the kingdom is in peril; again they are called to its deliverance. In ruined Cair Paravel, once their palace, they meet the good dwarf Trumpkin, who tells them that the rightful ruler, Prince Caspian, has had to flee from a usurper, and that he, with his tutor Doctor Cornelius, is hiding in the woods. Other dwarfs join them, and many good beasts. There is

Trufflehunter the badger and the endearing Bulgy Bears. There are moles, hares, owls, an ancient raven and Reepicheep, that "gay and valiant mouse". There come also the fauns and satyrs, Glenstorm the centaur with his sons, and an amiable giant.

Aslan also comes, and, strengthened by him, Peter overthrows the usurper in single combat. Prince Caspian is restored to this throne, many good people and beasts are set free, and Aslan raises to life an old, dying woman. "Oh, Aslan," she says, "I knew it was true; I've been waiting for this all my life." She thinks she could fancy a little breakfast. Bacchus, who has been in the triumphal procession, draws from the well a pitcher of wine "as red as red-current jelly, smooth as oil, strong as beef, warming as tea, cool as dew". The old woman had been nurse to the Prince and had been banished for telling him about the good days of the Narnian kings.

Aslan tells Susan and Peter that they will not come again to Narnia. They have grown too old. Lucy and Edmund will return once more. The children go back into their own world through a door in the wood and find themselves sitting on the station platform just as their trains are coming in.

In *The Voyage of the Dawn Treader*[54] Lucy and Edmund are accompanied, by no means to their delight, by their disagreeable cousin, Eustace. It is Aslan's will that he too should enter Narnia, and his conversion is part of the theme of the book. No long time has passed in Narnia. Caspian is King and he is unhappy about the fate of seven faithful lords, lost before the reign of the usurper. He has resolved to find them. Lucy, Edmund, the scoffing Eustace and Reepicheep sail with him on *The Dawn Treader* through strange seas to many islands. It is a little like *Gulliver's Travels*, but with none of Swift's fierce satire. The conversion of Eustace follows a catastrophe. On one island, exploring by himself, he enters a cave just as an ancient dragon dies. He finds a hoard of treasure, steals a bracelet and falls asleep. He awakens, enchanted into dragon form, having slept on dragon ground with dragon greed in his heart. Lucy and Edmund are full of pity for him, but they are helpless. Only Aslan can set him free. The great golden lion appears, strips off the dragon scales most painfully, and bids him bathe in a cool spring. The water cleanses him and heals his pain. There is spiritual cleansing too. This is his *metanoia*.

The voyage ends happily. Prince Caspian finds his friends,

and a Princess for his bride. For Reepicheep it is not the end of sea-faring. He must sail on by himself, in his coracle, until he comes to Aslan's own country. Before he sails, the children are granted a glimpse of that land. "What it brought them in that second," we are told, "none of these three children will ever forget. It brought both a smell and a musical sound." The boys would never speak of it. Lucy would say only that "it would break your heart", but this she said without sadness.

The three children land on a green shore to be welcomed by a white lamb who bids them come to breakfast. Fish is roasting on a fire. It is the most delectable food they have ever eaten. "Is this Aslan's country?" they ask, but the lamb tells them that they are not there yet. Their way thither must be from their own world. "There is a way into my country from all worlds," they are told. The lamb has become great and golden: it is Aslan.

"I am the great Bridge-builder," says he. For Lucy and Edmund there is now a farewell.

Eustace reappears, with a new companion, in the adventure of *The Silver Chair*[55]. His companion is Jill, a fellow pupil at his appalling school (on which the author pours vituperative scorn which slightly deflects the narrative). Many years have passed in Narnia. King Caspian is now old and feeble; his Queen is dead, by poison; their son Rilian is lost. From Trumpkin the dwarf and Glimfeather the owl Eustace and Jill hear all that has happened, all that they must now do to rescue Prince Rilian. In their quest they are helped by Puddleglum the Marsh-Wiggle, who is almost human in form, but grotesque. He is all arms and legs, mud-coloured and of dismal face and outlook, yet he is of heroic fortitude and endearing character. "I shouldn't wonder" is his usual opening remark, followed by a prediction of the worst that could happen. The children grow used to this pessimism, discover his virtue and loyalty and end by loving him. When Jill kisses him he is gratified but not overcome by surprise: "I *am* a good-looking chap," he muses.

The children find Prince Rilian held spellbound in the silver chair by the power of a witch even more evil than the Queen in *The Lion, the Witch and the Wardrobe*. At the height of their peril, Puddleglum offers the superb consolation that, if they were to die there, it would save funeral expenses.

There is, however, no need for any funeral. They overcome the witch, set Rilian free and return with him in joy, to be welcomed by the good people, the good beasts, the centaurs and the King himself. He can now say his *Nunc Dimittis* and depart in peace, having blessed his son. Aslan comes then, and shows the children the dead King lying in a clear, golden stream. They weep together for him, then Aslan bids Eustace pluck a thorn from a bush and pierce his paw. A drop of Aslan's blood, falling upon Caspian, restores him to life and to youth. He rises, strong and kingly, hailing Eustace as his comrade on that voyage long ago of *The Dawn Treader*. "In a very quiet voice, almost as if he were laughing," Aslan now tells the children that Caspian has indeed died in Narnia but that this is Aslan's country.

They may not stay longer, neither may they come again to Narnia until their final summons. Now they must go through the door into their own world and to the school which presently, by Aslan's unseen influence, is changed into a decent and tolerable place.

The fifth tale, *The Horse and His Boy*[56], is not closely linked with the others. In itself it is an excellent fairy-tale about Bree the horse who takes Shasta the boy away from the cruel land of Calormen into Narnia during the reign of High King Peter and Queen Susan, Queen Lucy and King Edmund.

In the sixth tale (in order of writing), *The Magician's Nephew*[57], we are taken back to the dawn, to the creation of Narnia; in our time, to the turn of the century, to the London of Sherlock Holmes and of E. Nesbit's Bastables. The boy Digory is living with an uncle and aunt in their suburban house. His father is in India; his mother lies gravely ill, almost at the point of death. He makes friends with Polly next door and they play in the garden and in the attic of Polly's house. There they discover a little door into the place which holds the cistern, and, beyond that, they tunnel under the roof, over the rafters, into Digory's house, where, finally, another little door opens into the forbidden room, his uncle's study. Uncle Andrew is, it appears, a magician dealing in malignant magic, a most unestimable character.

So begins the adventure of Polly and Digory which, half a century later, is to involve the Pevenseys, Eustace and Jill and bring them all to Narnia. The period setting is clear. George MacDonald would have delighted in that tunnel with the little door at each end and would have understood the malignity of Uncle Andrew.

The children come, by way of a deep pool, to a strange land and to a hall of images where kings and queens sit spellbound in royal splendour. After an unhappy quarrel, Digory (like any misguided character in fairy-tale) rings a bell which brings to life the most magnificent figure of all, Queen Jadis, the third of the witch-queens and most powerful and most evil of them all. Through Digory's act of petulant self-will comes much woe, but ultimate redemption through Aslan.

Queen Jadis follows the children to London and draws Uncle Andrew into her web of enchantment. From the hansom cab into which she has mounted, she transports Uncle Andrew, the children, the cabman and his horse into the primeval world from which, although they do not know it, Narnia is to be created. Fortunately the cabby is a heroic character. He could well be a grandson of Diamond's excellent father in *North Wind*. He is the sort of Londoner who rose to the height of courage during the blitz—which may have been in Lewis's mind.

"Keep cool, everyone," says the cabby in a moment of crisis. "If we've fallen down some diggings . . . someone will come and get us out . . . and if we're dead, well, a chap's got to die sometime, and there ain't nothing to be afraid of if a chap's led a decent life. . . The best thing we could do to pass the time would be to sing a 'ymn." He strikes up the only one he can remember, the harvest thanksgiving one about all being safely gathered in ere the winter's storms begin.

This good cabby, Frank, is with the children through their whole adventure. A voice is heard singing. To the children, Frank and his horse it is the most beautiful voice they have ever heard. To Jadis and the magician uncle it is a dreadful, hated sound. Light suddenly glows and the stars appear to be singing. A young sun rises and appears to laugh for joy. From the formless place rocks and hills and running water emerge; colour is seen, as well as light. The voice sings on, and the glorious golden lion appears. The singer is the *Vox Creatrix* "by whom all things were made". He sings into being the grass and tiny trees which quickly grow to full height, putting forth leaves. Finally he creates birds and beasts, great and small, and the tired old cab horse, suddenly grown young again, joins them.

"Narnia, Narnia," sings Aslan. "Love, speak, think. Be talking trees, be talking beasts, be divine waters."

It is the primal world, full of fun as well as beauty. "Laugh and fear not," Aslan bids them all. There are comical creatures there too. "Jokes as well as justice came in with speech." The jackdaw thinks he may have made the first joke, but Aslan tells him: "You have only *been* the first joke."

Frank the cabman is happy. Aslan seems to know and like him greatly. "I have known you long," he says.

"I feel somehow," replies Frank, "if I might make so free, as 'ow we've met before."

"You know better than you think," Aslan assures him. This is reminiscent of the dialogue in the Gospel between Christ the Judge and the humble blessed ones who had no idea that they were serving Him when they served their fellow men.

Digory confesses to Aslan his fault of ringing the bell in the hall of enchantment, and is forgiven. He is sent on a quest: he must find the tree of healing and bring back an apple which, planted in Narnia, will grow into a great tree and protect the kingdom for many golden years.

Digory tells Aslan, also, of his grief for his sick mother. "My son, my son," Aslan comforts him, "grief is great. Only you and I in this land know this yet. Let us be good to one another."

Aslan asks Frank if he will stay in Narnia as King. This Frank will gladly do if he may have his wife brought to him. Summoned by Aslan, she arrives, straight from her washing-tub, "surprised by joy" yet calm and self-possessed, seeming to find herself at home. She is a gentle woman. King Frank and Queen Helen will reign well and found a long line of good kings.

The cab horse, Strawberry, is transformed into a Pegasus with swift wings, and, renamed Fledge, he carries Digory and Polly to the far-off land where the tree of healing grows. There is a green valley ringed by mountains; in the heart of the valley there is a lake, beyond that a hill; at the top of the hill lies the garden where the apple tree grows.

Having plucked an apple, Digory is sorely tempted to take one for his mother as well, but he resists the temptation. Polly and he are carried back to Aslan, who plants the apple by a river of living water. Almost before they can see it grow, it is a great tree with branches that cast light rather than shadows and bear fruit bright as the stars. From that radiance the witch-queen Jadis flees in terror to the uttermost ends of the earth. Narnia is free and blessed.

Frank and Helen are crowned and they receive joyful homage from all their subjects. Aslan gives Digory an apple with his blessing. The children, with the deplorable but now helpless and harmless Uncle Andrew, are restored to their own time and place. Digory gives the apple, bit by bit, to his mother. She eats, smiles and falls into a natural, healing sleep. Digory plants the core in the garden.

Narnia now seems like a dream. But at home all is well—almost a miracle of happiness. Uncle Andrew becomes a tolerable character. Digory's mother recovers. His father inherits a fortune, comes home from India and buys a large country house. In the garden of their London home, the apple core grows into a tree bearing fruit more delicious than any other. "Inside itself, in the very sap of it, that tree never forgot that other tree in Narnia to which it belonged."

Digory and Polly do not forget Narnia, although they may not return to it. They guard their knowledge and memory well and their friendship endures. Digory, when he grows up, becomes a scholar. He is the Professor in whose house the four Pevenseys enter Narnia through a wardrobe—for that wardrobe is made from the wood of that apple tree after it had been blown down in a gale.

The Magician's Nephew is, in every way, a primal story. Though written sixth, it forms the foundation for all the others and it is itself a parable of creation, the beginning of a myth. All through these six tales we go in and out of Narnia; in the seventh and last, *The Last Battle*[58], we are, all through the action, out of this world.

Darkness has fallen upon the once bright kingdom of Narnia; there has been disaster beyond saving by any valiant defender. Tirian, the last of the kings, is held captive. The ancient foes of Narnia, the Calormenes, have taken the kingdom. They are led by the powerful Tash who is the embodiment of evil. His is a power beyond any hitherto encountered. His second in command is Rishda Tarkaan who has as his tool the malignant ape, Shift, who in turn has beguiled the poor ass Puzzle into serving him. The few talking beasts left in Narnia are helpless and the dwarfs have become selfish and ill willed.

King Tirian sees in a vision seven people round a table: an old man and woman of noble bearing and five young people. They are the Professor and Polly with Lucy, Peter, Edmund, Eustace and Jill. They see Tirian, for Aslan has begun to draw them back to Narnia to fight in the last battle. When they arrive and meet Tirian, Peter tells him why they are seven and not eight. Susan has fallen away, "having loved this present world". She has laughed at their talk and memories of Narnia, declaring them childish make-believe. Polly dismisses her: "She wasted all her school time wanting to be the age she is now, and she'll waste all the rest of her life trying to stay that age." Why is Susan treated in this way? There has been no preparation for her rejection of Narnia, no hint of weakness in her. She is given no chance to reform, to regain her childhood. It hurts us; it is bewildering, like the sudden disappearance, in *The Princess and Curdie,* of the Queen. It seems to indicate a loss of heart in the author.

The last battle is terrible beyond any other in Narnian history, but victory is won. Rishda Tarkaan and his creature the ape are destroyed by Tash, who has been called into Narnia. Poor Puzzle the donkey is spared. Tirian is free.

The victors gather in a stable which opens into a woodland. Lucy recalls that once in a stable something happened which was "bigger than our whole world". Aslan the judge appears, glorious and golden. He is merciful to the weak. He would have mercy on the dwarfs, but they are sullen and self-willed; they will have none of him and he will not compel them. To the good, even the feebly good, he is kind, and he welcomes one of the Calormenes, a youth who fought bravely for his own side until he realised its evil. Loyalty is itself good; this reformed disciple, having recognised a true fealty, is received among Aslan's own friends.

The seven tell Aslan how they have seemed to come to Narnia after a railway accident. They were all travelling to meet each other, and to meet the Pevenseys' parents, when there was a noise. "I felt very light," says Edmund. "Then here we are." The Professor and Polly no longer feel old. They see the end of Narnia, the dis-creation of all things. All Aslan's foes, Tash among them, are destroyed. Then all creation disappears: the stars fall from heaven to become star people and join the company in the stable; monsters devour the trees, then themselves shrivel and vanish; the giant, Time, squeezes the sun into a shred, into nothing; total darkness and formless chaos fall upon Narnia. This is the void out of which Polly and Digory had, long before, seen the kingdom created. This is the end: annihilation, dis-creation.

The company of the redeemed see it happen through the stable door, then they follow Aslan out into new light and loveliness. The children grieve for the loss of the Narnia they loved, but one of the good creatures, Farsight the eagle, tells them that Narnia still exists: he has seen it from a great height as he flew. This, Digory explains, is the true Narnia, of which the kingdom they have known is only a shadow and an image. In the same way, their own England is but a shadow of the real, eternal England they are now to find. This is a development of Newman's motto: "From shadows and images into truth."

The seven rush on together in happy procession, in something like the great Dance of the Blessed in Paradise. The children see their parents. They climb a waterfall to reach a fair, green place, recognised by Polly and Digory as the scene of the creation of Narnia. Beyond the waterfall stand golden gates which open to the peal of a horn. Beyond the gates they meet a host of old friends: Puddleglum the Marsh-Wiggle, Reepicheep the mouse, the good dwarf, the beavers, the fauns, the centaurs and, of course, Mr Tumnus, the first friend of all. There has been total redemption for all creatures with any good in them and with any will towards Aslan.

There is much talk and laughter. "You've no idea how good an old joke sounds when you take it out again after a rest of five or six hundred years."

In the centre of the paradisial garden sit King Frank and Queen Helen. "This garden is like the stable," says Lucy. "It is far bigger inside than it was outside."

To which Mr Tumnus replies, "The further up and the further in you go, the bigger everything gets. The inside is larger than the outside." It is a good description of myth and allegory.

Aslan now tells the children plainly that they are dead, killed, like their parents, in that railway crash. Now "the dream is over; this is the morning." They are in Aslan's own country and will never leave it.

Aslan is no longer a lion. What happens after this is impossible to relate. They have begun the story "which no-one on earth has ever read, which goes on for ever; in which every chapter is better than the one before."

Chapter 12

THE TREE OF FAIRY-TALE

J. R. R. Tolkien and *Fairy Stories*

"Faerie is a perilous land. . . I have been hardly more than a wandering explorer (or trespasser) in the land, full of wonder but not of information."

That self-description, given in Tolkien's lecture, *Fairy Stories,* is a masterpiece of self-depreciation and under-statement. No-one since Robert Kirk has gone further into those perilous realms or brought us clearer news than Professor Tolkien. It is proper that one who was both scholar and maker should transform a lecture into a creative art form simply by stating facts. But the facts are, of course, unusual. Tolkien's talk was the Andrew Lang Lecture of 1938, given at the University of St Andrews. His was a most suitable subject, dealing with one of Lang's most cherished interests.

The lecture, *Fairy Stories,* has been reprinted with Tolkien's story of Leaf and Niggle, its new title being *Tree and Leaf*[59]. The image contained in the title is appropriate, for the lecture seems to grow like a tree bearing leaves and fruit. It is like the tree which grew from Digory's apple core, which remembered its source in Narnia and which had made from its wood one of the entrances to that kingdom.

Most fairy-tales deal with the wanderings and adventures of men drawn into the realm of faery by magic compulsion or their own intense desire (if these two are not really one). The inhabitants of faery are not, Tolkien maintains, "primarily concerned with us nor we with them". We are two races apart from each other, hence the peril of our entering their world. This agrees with Robert Kirk's account.

The nature of faery, "the wind that blows in that country", cannot be described or defined. It is conveyed by old legends and ballads like *Thomas the Rhymer,* by poems like *Kilmeny* and by tales like *Sir Gawain and the Green Knight,* which holds both

101

realism and magic and has a clarity of background and atmosphere.

In discussing the various types of fairy-tale, Tolkien gives tepid praise to the courtly French stories of Perrault and Madame d'Aulnoy. The dream-sequence he rejects altogether for its exclusion of "the realisation of imagined wonder". He insists that, "It is essential to a genuine fairy-tale that it be presented as true." This definition must exclude *Alice in Wonderland* and *Through the Looking-Glass* which Tolkien in childhood found amusing but not entrancing. They did not stir any wonder.

To be presented as true, and as having happened out of our time and our world, is a test triumphantly passed by the old tales of adventures in faery, by the best Victorian fantasies and by those of our own day. Diamond did not dream of the North Wind and her country, neither did the Princess and Curdie dream of the Queen in her attic—Curdie, indeed, did not see her as she really was until he awoke. The Ardens went back into the past of their own family and Dickie returned there to end his life—he was more alert, more awake than his cousins. The magic was a dream only in so far as all that happens in this life is just a dream, before we awaken to eternal reality. The four Pevenseys went into Narnia and came out again by Aslan's bidding. It was a real journey with real adventure, and, when Susan in adolescent folly chose to think it make-believe, she was forever banished. These other worlds, reached by magic, have reality and realism.

Tolkien would not have counted Beatrix Potter's books as fairy-tales, which judgement may, however reluctantly, be conceded, for once we have accepted the fact that her animals wear clothes, sit at table to eat their meals and talk to each other in human speech, there is no magic: they are in their true form and behave according to their nature. Mrs Tiggy-Winkle really washes and irons the clothes, she does not mutter a spell. Only in one story, *The Tailor of Gloucester*, do the mice come with magic help for their human friend.

It is difficult to agree to the exclusion of *The Wind in the Willows*, even if Rat, Mole, Badger and the rest are not enchanted into their way of life, living in houses, with human habits, speech and friendships, for the air of faery is fresh and sweet throughout the book. Tolkien says of mythology that it holds some "divinity, the right to power . . . the due of worship, in fact, *religion*", and that is a precise description of the scene where Rat and Mole find and worship Pan.

In all good fairy-tales there is sound morality, but the moral must neither thrust itself assertively out of the story nor be an obvious addition. It should be part of the structure, part of the essense of the story, as it is in the primal narrative of creation: "Thou shalt not . . ." eat of this fruit, or open this door, or move hand or foot. The breaking of a command or prohibition traditionally brings some catastrophe, and every fault must be expiated.

Like Lewis, Tolkien refuses to limit the audience for fairy-tales to children. This form can appeal to all minds, the mature and scholarly as well as the young and unformed. It is bread and wine, not milk and sweets and such nursery fare. Children are, after all, not a separate creation, a different kind of creature, but members, however immature, of the human family. Not all children enjoy fairy-tales any more than they all care for music or poetry, for puzzles or for outdoor games. Those who do appreciate them are fortunate, as are the grown-ups who share this love. Such people have a new dimension added to their knowledge, and they find a new delight in "the willing suspension of unbelief". A tale of marvels well told compels belief, which is an assent of the will.

The story-teller is, in Tolkien's word, a "sub-creator", creating a separate world where marvels may happen and be accepted if they are in accord with the laws of that world. There must be an artistic compulsion, drawing the reader or the hearer within that new creation.

Tolkien as a child loved dragons: dragons in their own realm, certainly not in this. Children usually delight in fantastic perils and terrors, enjoying them as long as they are assured that the monsters involved cannot invade their own real world. Dragons, giants, wizards—the whole *clamjamfry* (to use a good Scots word) are credible, even desirable, citizens of that sub-creation. The more evil they are, the better the adventure and keener the excitement. Children must merely be assured that none of the creatures is lurking about the house.

Tolkien finds four elements essential to fairy-tale: Fantasy, Recovery, Escape and Consolation. Fantasy includes "image-making". In all the strangeness and wonder, some discipline must be imposed on the imagination; a predetermined form must be accepted. Faery has its own laws to which Fantasy must be obedient. "Art", writes Tolkien, "is the human process that reproduces secondary belief"—belief, that is, in the faery realm and its laws. Fantasy neither denies fact nor attacks reason. "We have the right to enter this sub-creation of fantasy because we are made in the image and likeness of a Creator." Our desire is pure and profound, clean of the magician's greed which would use magic for selfish ends.

Once, when challenged by a critic who held all fantasy to be mere lies, Tolkien replied in verse:

> Man is not wholly lost nor wholly changed,
> *Dis*-graced he may be, yet is not dethroned,
> And keeps the rags of lordship once he owned.

Man as sub-creator reflects the divine light; he creates to the glory of God. It is the better part of our fallen nature which finds solace and delight in fairy-tales. MacDonald said that too:

> The house is not for me, it is for Him.
> His royal thoughts require many a stair,
> Many a tower, many an outlook fair
> Of which I have no thought.

And the Divine Owner of the house welcomes many a guest.

To see the truth in Fantasy we need Recovery: a recovery of sight and insight, of a healthy imagination; a recovery which can come only from humility.

"We should look at green again, and be startled anew (but not blinded) by blue and yellow and red," wrote Tolkien. We should meet fairy-tale centaurs and dragons and then discover, really discover, dogs and sheep and horses. This was Chesterton's assertion too. Fairy-tales can be wholesome medicine: healing herbs, purifying mind and imagination (as *Phantastes* did for C. S. Lewis). They can bring renewal, soundness of mental health, wholeness and wholesomeness which comes close to holiness. "It was in fairy-tales", says Tolkien, "that I first divined the potency of the words and the wonder of the things, such as stone and wood and iron; tree and grass; house and fire; bread and wine."

After Recovery comes Escape, which is no evasion of reality, no running away from unendurable pain or from mere boredom and monotony. Dislike of ugliness is not cowardice; the squalor of many a town is, after all, no more real than the beauty of a pastoral landscape. There is a sensible, resourceful, even heroic kind of escape, as when prisoners of war evade their captors and make their way back to freedom at great risk; there is the fundamental and righteous desire to escape from exile to one's own country; there is the desire to return to a country of innocence and goodness. The fantasy of comradeship between men and talking birds and beasts is part of this desire for innocence, of this sort of escape, because, traditionally, such friendships were known in Eden. Kilmeny found this innocence again and brought it back with her to this world for a time. In this desire to escape there is contrition for our sins against the animals and for our share in the flaw of nature. Escape may be a way of expiation.

Deepest of all is the longing for "the great Escape" from death. This is the theme of much of George MacDonald's fantasy. The way may be through the death of the body, a good death leading to eternal life.

Finally, after Escape comes Consolation, the happy ending. To desire this is right, and it must be defended against any charge of weakness or sentimentality. We *should* demand that all will be well in the end. It is the Christian expectation. In fairy-tale there is the *eucatastrophe,* the reversal of the catastrophe which appeared for a time to overwhelm the good characters.

The heroine in *The Black Bull of Norroway* must, for her very small fault of forgetfulness, serve seven years, make a weary journey and find herself tricked and nearly bereft again of her love. Then comes the eucatastrophe of his awakening and recognition.

There may come a sudden deliverance which is like the miracle of forgiveness and divine grace. The eucatastrophe is real joy, which is beyond, even different from, mere happiness. It does not deny sorrow and failure, for these are necessary to the joy of deliverance. After defeat comes the evangel of succour and salvation, the good news, a radiance "beyond the walls of the world, poignant as grief" but cancelling grief. "It would break your heart," Lucy said of that glimpse of Aslan's country they had in *The Dawn Treader,* long before the final battle and victory and their coming to that country. She did not mean that it was sorrowful.

The eucatastrophe is sudden, but it is certain. Dante coming up out of hell beheld the stars, then the *dolce color zaffiro;* he did not return to the infernal darkness. When it comes, the eucatastrophe brings "a beat and lifting of the heart near to (or indeed accompanied by) tears". Joy is the mark of the fairy-tale as it is of the most glorious of all tales, the Gospels. Joy is Revelation.

Tolkien develops his theme: "God redeemed the corrupt making-creatures, men, in a way fitting to this aspect. . . The Gospels contain a fairy story . . . which embraces all the essence of fairy-stories." They are full of marvels and miracles culminating in the supreme eucatastrophe of the Resurrection. But this marvellous story happened in this world, within history, in one particular place and period of our time. "The birth of Christ", wrote Tolkien, "is the eucatastrophe of man's history. The Resurrection is the eucatastrophe of the Incarnation. The story begins and ends in joy."

The disciples and the faithful women knew that sudden turn to joy when they came to the empty tomb, or when they saw a guest at supper break bread, or when they were bidden to a breakfast by the lakeside. This story belongs to the primary world, to creation, not to the world of sub-creation, however lovely that may be and however clear a reflection it is of the primary world. It is supreme "and it is true. Art has been verified. God is the Lord of the angels and of men—and of elves. Legend and History have met and fused."

So, Lewis brought the fauns and centaurs and all the good talking beasts, together with the children, into Aslan's country. George MacDonald saw the good dogs and horses climb the stair to heaven with the Little Ones, and go off to their celestial stalls and fields. They are all sharers in the eucatastrophe.

Chapter 13

THE NORTHERN NOBILITY

Tolkien and *Beowulf*

In his childhood Tolkien loved the myths and legends of the north such as *Sigurd the Volsung* and many a tale of dragons and dragon-slayers. Like C. S. Lewis he discovered "northernness". Perhaps he discovered it sooner and more easily, for he *was* northern, being Danish by descent, while his scholarship was Anglo-Saxon and Scandinavian rather than classical and Mediterranean. In him, as in Lewis, the scholar and maker are one, perfectly fused.

John Ronald Reuel Tolkien, born in 1892, went from King Edward's School, Birmingham, to Exeter College, Oxford. He became Reader, then Professor of English Language at Leeds, then returned to Oxford as Professor of Anglo-Saxon. He edited many early English classics, including *The Pearl, The Ancrene Wisse* and *Sir Gawain and the Green Knight,* that most northern of all the Arthurian romances with its own blending of magic and realism. In this one classic, two of Tolkien's childish loves were satisfied: that for tales about King Arthur and that for northernness.

If the lecture on *Fairy-Stories* is a key to the inmost room in Tolkien's castle of the mind, that on *Beowulf: the Monsters and the Critics,* given to the British Academy in 1936, is hardly less important as a clue to his creative art. As poet and story-teller, this scholar defends *Beowulf* against those critics who lay upon the poem a burden it was not meant to bear; those who would make it "a heathen, heroic lay, a history of Sweden, a manual of German antiquities or a Nordic *Summa Theologica*". Tolkien himself knew what a poem could and should be. *Beowulf* is a myth, related by a poet who "feels rather than makes explicit what his theme portends".

Such a narrative gives delight, even while unbelief is not wholly suspended. "The proud we"—the intellectual—may find the ogres, monsters and dragons "a mad mistake", but they are necessary to the myth. Within the realm of myth, dragons and other monsters are desirable; they are strange and strong creatures of the imagination. Tolkien refers to the need for recovery, for a renewed clearness of vision. This is necessary before entering the realm of myth and magic. It is a quality of mind not always found in critics. A place for dragons, and dragons in their place, is a sound rule.

The hero Beowulf himself is first victorious and then defeated, but he is finally triumphant. All the time he is heroic. He is at war with evil: he may be overthrown in the temporal combat, but not in eternity. The human conflict can be tragic. Grendel, his mother and the other monsters are essential to the tragedy in the same way that Tolkien's own creatures of dreadful power and evil in his epic myth *Lord of the Rings* are essential to that narrative of power, terror and splendour.

Beowulf has been called "almost a Christian knight". Tolkien prefers to say that he moves in "a northern, heroic age imagined by a Christian, and therefore has a noble and gentle quality, although himself a pagan". Like any Christian knight he is fighting the enemies of God. In the poet's imagination the Christian and the heroic pagan elements have fused. The poem, Tolkien thinks, probably belongs to the age of Bede, who was himself aware of the old world and the old faith, "who saw both the twilight and the dawn".

Tolkien's own imagination also holds this unity. Himself Christian and Catholic, he did not think ill of the heroic pagans and their gods. Although he did not present total redemption as clearly as does Lewis, it is there in his mind, in his imagination and his sub-creation.

There is, in *Beowulf*, the great northern virtue of courage, finding expression in endurance as well as in active heroism. In the Norse and the early English sagas, gods and mortals fight together against evil and against the monsters. These gods are not difficult to reconcile with the new faith: they are not corrupt; they have nobility. They are sad, even hopeless when the fight goes against them, but in that very sadness there is valour. Though defeat may overwhelm both gods and men, such defeat is temporal. Even though the world may end in darkness and dissolution, eternal victory lies beyond. In *Beowulf* there is a hint, a glimmer of the eucatastrophe.

There is *pietas* in *Beowulf*: that old, strong virtue which cherishes the good of the past and which is loyal to right tradition, carrying it towards the future. There is something of expectation, almost the sense of Advent. Tolkien finds the same quality in *The Aeneid*, the supreme poem of the borderland between the old faith and the new. Virgil, like the unknown Christian maker of the Anglo-Saxon *Beowulf*, conveys the sense "of many-storied antiquity, together with its natural accompaniment, stern and noble melancholy". These two would appear to stand one on either side of the threshold of the Christian revelation, almost as if they stood at the door of the stable where something greater than the whole world once happened.

The Norse gods have, for Tolkien, a human quality, a poignancy, lacking in those of Greece and Rome. Like men, they live in time and in the expectation of death. "Baldur the beautiful is dead." His death brings grief to the gods in Asgard and they are thereby closer to men.

Beowulf is, in Tolkien's description, less an epic than an elegy, almost a dirge. There is a cosmic element in it. "We look down as if from a visionary height upon the house of man in the valley of the world"—a house like the hall in the poem, made lively with music, lights and feasting, while, outside in the darkness, Grendel prowls, hateful and terrifying. There is terror in the poem. It is tragic, but it is full of the old fortitude, with a glimmer of the new Christian light.

"The mythology of a people is far more than a collection of pretty or terrifying fables. . . It is the comment of the men of one particular age or civilisation on the mysteries of human existence and the human mind . . . their attempt to define, in stories of gods and demons, their perception of the inner realism." Thus Dr Hilda Ellis Davidson begins her study of *Gods and Myths of Northern Europe*[60]. Delight in myth is not a desire to escape from drab reality, it is a humble search after knowledge and understanding. This matches Tolkien's defence of fairy-tale and his idea of Escape. And, like Tolkien, Dr Davidson stresses the northern virtues of courage, honour and integrity. There is also a respect for women. The high goddesses, the queens and great ladies are held in honour. Loyalty reaches beyond the grave: the heroic dead are remembered. This is *pietas*. All these virtues prepare the entrance of the new faith. And the virtues of compassion for the weak and an infinite capacity for forgiveness are essentially Christian.

The northern gods, when not engaged in conflict, are genial. Odin the Wanderer loves to go about in disguise, meeting ordinary folk, hearing their talk and discovering their way of life. Tolkien has put a good deal of him into Gandalf the Grey, the wanderer and wizard who summons Bilbo in *The Hobbit* and Frodo in *The Fellowship of the Ring* on their quest and adventure, and who is himself one of the leading characters in both tales.

The emblem of the tree Yggdrasil in northern mythology recurs in modern myths. It grows at the heart of the world and has three roots: one in the above of the giants, one in the realm of the dead and one in Aesir, the dwelling of the descendants of the gods. This is found in Tolkien's trilogy and it is the source of the tree magic, for good or evil, in George MacDonald.

The Scot was not so much an influence on Tolkien as an affinity, a spiritual father. MacDonald and Tolkien speak and know the same language. There is a third in their company: William Morris, because of his love of northernness and the nature of some of his romances.

Morris visited Iceland in 1871 and was almost, in the fairy sense of the word, *translated:* taken into a new world, the sense and memory of which would not leave him. He wrote about his riding to a river which ran through a "soft, grassy plain". "It was wonderfully clear, and its flowery green lips . . . quite beautiful to me in the sunny evening, though I think at any time I should have liked the place, with the grass and sea and river all meeting, and the great black mountain on the other side of the firth."

It was a setting for legend. The reality was homely: he was given a genial welcome and enjoyed hospitality, rides and expeditions. Yet the visit left an impression of melancholy.

Morris was sensitive to the contrast between the forgotten, heroic past and the comfortable, even smug present. There was sadness in his mind, relieved by ecstasy. The Icelandic landscape inspired him: he found it "a melancholy, beautiful and solemn place" where "all the infinite wonder comes on me again". There was to be an element of dread in his feeling: it haunted him. And the memory of it lies within his romances of quest and wandering.

Lewis loved Morris and has written of his delight in his "watercolour world" and his medieval and Norse tales. Would it be an exaggeration to see in this journey to Iceland a spiritual experience for Morris, a re-birth, such as Lewis found in reading George MacDonald? There was no such need of *metanoia* or of baptism for Morris as there was, by his own confession, for Lewis; but there was a need for a certain discipline, for astringency. Morris's later romances, *The Wood Beyond the World* and *The Well at the World's End,* are still told in his typical coloured prose (too much Morris's own creation to be a mere *pastiche* of medieval style, yet over-rich, over-jewelled for some tastes), nevertheless, the tales hold us and compel us to read. Behind the richness lies realism, like a landscape of river and forest, which knows darkness and storm as well as sunlight, lying beyond the windows of a hall hung with tapestry and richly furnished. In Iceland, Morris awoke to a new vision, not without dread. "The cliffs were . . . most unimaginably strange," he wrote, "they had caves in them just like the hell-mouths in thirteenth-century illuminations. . . The great mountain wall which closes up the valley, with its jagged outlying teeth, was right before us now, looking quite impassable. . . More often, the wall would be cleft, and you would see a horrible winding street with stupendous straight rocks for houses on either side." When he could see the whole length of the mountain wall, with many waterfalls dripping from glaciers and the black valley beneath, he felt "cowed, and as if I should never get back again; yet with that came a feeling of exultation too."

Morris's awakening also led many years later to *The Wood Beyond the World, The Water of the Wondrous Isles* and *The Well at the World's End,* of which Lewis said that no story could ever match the magic of that last title.

Chapter 14

HOBBITS AND HEROES

I
The Beginning

It began with the tale of a hobbit in his hole[61], told by Tolkien to his children, who gave approval, encouragement, criticism or advice as seemed proper and where seemed desirable. This beginning was homely, even cosy—and it created a new race.

Elves, fauns and fairies have always been with us, but hobbits are new. They are not of faery and they have no magic powers "except the ordinary everyday sort which helps them to disappear quietly and quickly". Like the Good People, they prefer to keep themselves to themselves. Although they bear no ill will to human beings, they have no need of them. A large, self-contained and highly competent community, they would not dream of stealing a human child or nurse.

Hobbits live in hobbit-holes, which are very far from being mere dens or burrows. They are, like the houses of the Good People in Robert Kirk's account, "large and fair", warm, clean and well-furnished: what is known in Scotland as *bien*, with an ample plenishing of linen, food and clothes.

Most hobbits are well-to-do. In fact, far from being uncanny, strange or fantastic creatures, they would seem to be solid, respectable and even a little dull—until, of course, things begin to happen. In appearance they are small but well-proportioned and they dress well, liking bright colours and rich materials. Their only difference from human beings in form is that they have furry feet and wear no shoes.

They do not, by any means, live upon the mere essence of food like the elves, fauns and fairies; they like their meals to be as frequent and as solid as possible, with plenty to drink. A genial people, they relish good talk and stories and they laugh a lot with "deep fruity laughs (especially after dinner which they have twice a day when they can get it)". Naturally they tend to be rather fat, and they take life easily. Highly respectable and settled in their ways, they have no desire for adventure and the unexpected; in normal circumstances they would not dream of setting forth upon a quest.

Among the hobbits, one of the most respected and comfortable is Mr Bilbo Baggins, a member of one of the largest families in the Shire, as their region is called. He is very well pleased with himself and his condition. But Bilbo, on his mother's side, is a Took, and the Tooks are a somewhat different family. They are tinged with imagination, with a feeling for the unusual. They are like a good middle-class human family who have every now and then produced someone out of the ordinary—a poet, a musician, an artist or an explorer. For most of the time Bilbo is more Baggins than Took, but heredity is an odd thing.

To him one day comes Gandalf the Grey, wanderer and wise man, with a summons to go on a journey far beyond his ordered world, which will put an end, for many a day, to his secure and cosy life in his excellent house under the hill. At first Bilbo will not listen. Then the dwarves arrive: a host of them cooly hanging up their hoods in the hall, making themselves at home and expecting supper. They are at first no great problem, for Bilbo is a hospitable fellow with a well-stocked larder and cellar. But then they begin to be too much for him. They are hearty eaters and by the end of the evening there is not much left in the larder. Supper is followed by singing, and then by a council which is the most disturbing thing of all.

The dwarves tell Bilbo about a lost treasure, guarded by a dragon, which must be recovered. It would be a grand fireside tale if it were only that, but as a summons it is not so inviting. Bilbo goes wearily to bed and awakens next morning to a house deserted by its recent company. The place is in complete disorder, with piles of unwashed dishes and glasses. It is the worst kind of morning after the night before. But no sooner has Bilbo washed up and restored some semblance of order than in walks Gandalf. And this time he must be obeyed. Reluctantly Bilbo sets out to follow the dwarves and share with them the journey and the quest.

Gradually there comes the change noted by Lewis. The humour, the realism and the "sheer hobbitry" are never lost, but there is a new dimension, another ambience. Soon Bilbo faces real peril and formidable adversaries. There is dread. Yet he is only an ordinary hobbit. Or is he? This becomes a tale not only of adventure and danger and victory, but of *metanoia*. Bilbo is not converted from a bad to a good hobbit—he has always been a very decent one—but he is changed into something like a hero. As Lewis has said, it is like passing from *The Wind in the Willows* to a Norse saga. But it should be added that the hero of the saga is no great warrior. Bilbo remains himself even at the crisis of peril, and when he returns to the Shire he may be somewhat changed but he is still very much a hobbit.

The story has the four essential fairy-tale elements: Fantasy, Recovery, Escape and Consolation. Bilbo emerges from his life of comfort, from a snugness which comes near smugness, when he sets forth on that fateful morning. He escapes not into peace and security but into heroism, and after much suffering he finds consolation. The initial fantasy of the hobbit world which begins the story is never lost. The fascination of the story lies not only in the continual and increasing excitement and mounting tension but also in the gradual change, the *metanoia*, experienced by Bilbo. Although he discovers both terror and beauty far beyond anything in hobbitry, and beyond anything he has ever imagined, he is capable of receiving both.

Most of Bilbo's journey is made with the dwarves, who are good comrades, but when the first crisis comes it is a solitary combat with Gollum, that strange and loathsome creature who lurks in the depths of the goblins' cave and addresses himself as "Precious". Although small and thin, he is horrifying of aspect, with enormous eyes like lamps, they being the only point of light in his dark cavern. There is a contest of wits that Bilbo only just wins and from which he barely escapes.

When Bilbo rejoins the dwarves, they have a series of adventures on their journey through Murkwood where they are captured by the mischievous wood-elves. Bilbo frees them eventually and they float down-river in wine-casks to Laketown. But then all comedy vanishes, Bilbo and the dwarves, helped by the people of the lake, reach the Lonely Mountain and arouse the dragon, Smaug, who, in an act of violent retribution, destroys Laketown before being killed himself by a single arrow. The treasure is safe and the mountain freed from its tyranny of greed and fear. But the final peril is yet to come in the Battle of Five Armies in which the irresponsible wood elves, the eagles of the forest, Beorn the bear man,

Gandalf, the dwarves and the survivors of Laketown fight to the death with the evil goblins and their allies, the wolf Wargs. It is a fierce and terrible battle in which many are slain, ending in the rout of the goblins and a strange new peace over the land. Finally Bilbo returns with Gandalf to the Shire, taking his share of the treasure and the ring he found in Gollum's cave.

The old, easy life is resumed—but with a difference. The comforts of food, fire, possessions and security are now more keenly relished than before, and there is a new zest for life, a sense of the unusual and a knowledge of a wider world beyond the Shire. Bilbo has also made new friends. Sometimes he goes to visit the Elves, and his inner life is so enriched that he takes to writing poetry. The Took in him is now stronger than the Baggins.

The ending is most satisfying for it leaves a window wide open towards other lands and further adventures. In this end a beginning is almost apparent.

And the new beginning occurs in the great saga which grew from this fairy-tale: *The Lord of the Rings*. Bilbo is like Thomas the Rhymer who returned home from Elfland for a time, but for whom a second summons came. By the end of *The Hobbit* there has already been the change in Bilbo which prepares us for what is to come.

II

Apotheosis of a Hobbit

Tolkien's saga, *The Lord of the Rings*, like *The Hobbit*, opens with a homely scene[62]: a family feast to celebrate the birthdays of Bilbo and his nephew and heir, Frodo. After the festivities Bilbo departs, though no-one knows where. Many years pass until one day Gandalf comes to warn Frodo that the ring Bilbo found in the grim tunnels of the goblins' lair, and now left to Frodo with Bilbo's other possessions, is the most powerful of all the rings of old and is, at that very moment, being sought by its creator, Sauron, the Dark Lord of Mordor. Frodo must flee because if Sauron recovers the ring Middle Earth will be overwhelmed by a force so evil and fierce that even the combined magic of the white wizards would shrink before it.

Frodo, like Bilbo long before him, is reluctant to obey the call.

Life in the Shire is very pleasant this fine spring-tide. Gandalf talks to him in the study where the window is open to the garden; the sun is warm and everything is fresh and fragrant, with "the new green of spring . . . shimmering in the fields and on the tips of the trees' fingers". He does not wish to leave this delectable world. Gandalf tells him of the ring and of the other rings, of

One Ring to rule them all, One Ring to find them,

One Ring to bring them all and in the darkness bind them.

The journey before Frodo is daunting beyond anything faced by Bilbo, but Frodo obeys the warning and leaves, taking with him his gardener, Sam Gamgee, who was working outside the window while Gandalf spoke of the quest. He listened without scruple and resolved to follow his master, joining this Fellowship of the Ring. To them are added two young hobbits, Merry Brandybuck and Pippin Took.

So, the fantasy of the hobbit world continues. Escape from security has come, and the beginning of a recovery of a sense of high adventure. Consolation will be long in bringing them joy, but there are delightful interludes.

The Hobbit is enchanting in its warmth and homeliness, its humour and excitement, and *The Fellowship of the Ring*, though greater, is not different, for it grows from that little seed, and the small tale has all the promise of the great, like the prelude to an opera. But, in magnitude of theme, depth of imagination and austere beauty of style, *The Fellowship* is seldom surpassed in modern literature. Tolkien's praise of *Beowulf* could also be applied to his own work. One could say that it has "an unrecapturable magic . . . for those who have ears to hear, profound feeling and poignant vision, filled with the beauty and mortality of the world". It is full of northern splendour.

Frodo retains for a while that hobbit homeliness which Sam, Merry and Pippin never lose, but he grows in dignity, achieving something like Elfin nobility, and rises to his own unique heroism. There is a *metanoia* in him even greater than in Bilbo.

As the four hobbits go on their way, they sing their song:

Farewell we call to hearth and hall;
Though wind may blow and rain may fall,
We must away ere break of day,

Far over wood and mountain tall
To Rivendell where elves yet dwell
In glades beneath the misty fell,
Through moor and waste we ride in haste
And whither then we cannot tell.

Early in their journey they come to a place of refreshment and delight, a foretaste, as it were, of the final Consolation. They come there after their first encounter with evil. Pippin and Merry were caught in the wood by the Willow, an evil tree, and to their rescue had come Tom Bombadil, singing a song which compelled the tree to release them. Tom is a character as old as the hills and woods and rivers, as young as spring and the new leaves. He is elemental, not wholly of faery, not wholly (or at all) human, although of human form and speech. He lives in a goodly house, eating excellent food, enjoying fire and warmth. He is tall but not gigantic, comely, kind and full of ancient wisdom.

MacDonald and Morris would both have recognised him as someone similar to their own creations and even more would they have welcomed his wife, the naiad Goldberry. This episode would have had illustrations by Arthur Rackham, had time not made the sad division of death.

As the hobbits follow Tom they hear a voice singing, a voice "as young and as ancient as spring", with the sound of water flowing "from a bright morning in the hills". Goldberry, although a daughter of the river, is of no cold or unearthly beauty: she is lovely, kind and warm and her house if full of comfort and welcome. She is sitting, all in green and silver, with great earthenware bowls of water-lilies at her feet, and comes to welcome the friends. Her table is spread with delectable food, with bread and butter, cheese, honey, fruit and cream. To such a house Birdalone might have come from the water of the Wondrous Isles, having found help and protection in Habundia, the lady of the wood; or Ralph in his quest for the well at the world's end. But Tolkien's magic is stronger than Morris's, however lovely that may be.

There is, in this first adventure, the quick rescue, the immediate solace and the lovely homeliness to reassure us. The hobbits sleep that night in a room all green and yellow, each provided with a pair of green slippers, and they sleep soundly and refreshingly. They waken to the sound of rain and spend all next day by the fireside listening to Tom Bombadil's talk. His words "laid bare the hearts of trees and their thoughts which were often dark and strange and filled with a hatred of things that go free upon the earth. . . It was not called the Old Forest for nothing. . . In it there lived, though ageing no quicker than the hills, the fathers of fathers of trees, remembering the time when they were lords." Some of them have grown in pride and malice, others in wisdom. Of them all, the Willow is most evil. "His heart was rotten, but his strength was green. . . His grey, thirsty spirit drew power out of the earth."

Tom has many tales of the earth as well as of the trees, of the ancient kings, and of ghosts and "barrow-wights" who dwell in tombs and hollows and are powerful in evil. He can remember all the ages of the earth: the first rain-drop, the first acorn. He was there before the river and the trees. He saw the coming of the Little People. "He is Master of wood, water and hills," Goldberry has told them, but he does not own these things: all things growing belong to themselves.

Tom warns the hobbits. He knows how darkness and evil have arisen; he knew the earth in her innocence, knew "the dark under the stars when it was fearless, before the Dark Lord came from outside".

There is an echo of northern myths here, and of the sort of menace Anados feels in *Phantastes* when he wanders in the wood and encounters the evil trees, it is the strange darkness which Morris felt in Iceland.

"Keep to the green grass," is Tom's final warning, and away from "cold stone and barrow-wights". He teaches them a song which will bring him to their aid, and it is not long before they must use it. Frodo is trapped by a barrow-wight, but he does not lose hope or courage. As he fights his terror in the darkness, he sees a light, and that light comes from himself. He is unflawed. Frodo hears a cold, cruel voice crying, The night was railing against the morning of which it was bereaved, and the cold was cursing the warmth for which it hungered. This is the primeval discord and horror, the hatred of corruption for the good light and for the warmth and cleanness it has lost. Frodo sees an arm reach out to seize his three comrades. He knows that he himself could escape by power of the ring he carries, but he resists the temptation to save only himself. He draws his sword and cuts off the outstretched hand. There is a shriek and the sword splinters.

Then he sings the summoning song:

> Ho, Tom Bombadil, Tom Bombadillo,
> By water, wood and hill, by the reed and willow,
> By fire, sun and moon, hearken now and hear us;
> Come, Tom Bombadil, for our need is near us.

A light glimmers. Tom's voice replies; he appears singing a rune against the barrow-wight:

> Shrivel like the cold mist, like the winds go wailing . . .
> Come never here again! leave your barrow empty!
> Lost and forgotten be, darker than the darkness
> Where gates stand forever shut, till the world is mended.

There is another long, terrible shriek; then silence. Tom and Frodo carry the three small hobbits out to the air and Tom revives them. Before they set forth again he gives to each a dagger forged by men hostile to the Dark Lord.

They ride on to the inn at Bree where they are menaced by the Dark Riders and meet one, Strider, a wanderer, who warns them of further peril and gives them news of Gandalf. He then reveals himself as no vagrant, but as a great Lord, Aragorn.

There follows a capital cloak-and-dagger episode. The Dark Riders attack and Frodo is nearly slain. But the enemies are overthrown; they fall into the river and are drowned. The Elf-lord Glorfindel appears and conducts Aragorn and the hobbits to the house of Elrond, Lord of Rivendell, where they once again find Gandalf. Here they rest and are feasted. Elrond is noble and venerable, old and yet ageless. With him is his daughter Arwen, "the evenstar of her people", lately returned from her mother's land of Lorien. She is of starlike beauty, her eyes full of wisdom. "Such loveliness in living thing Frodo had never seen before nor imagined." This new sight is part of his Recovery. He sees a vision of pure beauty which he adores selflessly. In this, too, is something of Consolation, a promise of what is to come at the end.

There is a recurrent contrast between beauty and delight on the one hand and horror and danger on the other. But Tolkien's characters are engaged in a deadlier conflict, a conflict with primal evil. In Morris we move between two worlds, one of faery, the other of medieval England as he imagined it. The enchantments are potent enough, but we know them to be enchantments, like those of the old fairy-tales. We are never in doubt as to the ending. We know that the hero and heroine will overcome the witches and wizards with all their spells and that they will come safely home and live happily ever after. But the strength of evil in Tolkien's myth can shake and daunt us almost to the end. We have in his created world, as in this life, a faith that in the end all will be well, but that faith is often difficult to hold. We are engulfed by his world; we are not merely looking at it.

With the strength of evil in Tolkien goes a spiritual beauty which is beyond the loveliest enchantment in any fairy-tale. It is something beyond the clearest and richest vision of Morris. It may be just to say that Morris depicts an earthly paradise whereas Tolkien, like Dante, takes us from the borders of Hell, through Purgatory, to that high region where, purgation ended, we are in sight of the true Paradise. And Tolkien's affinity with Morris ends with the end of this first volume of the trilogy.

In the house of Elrond the hobbits are called to council and they are joined by a new comrade, Boromir, the human Prince of Gondor. The Fellowship of the Ring is formed. The fellows are told about their adversary, Sauron, Lord of the Rings of Power, Lord of Evil. Gandalf recites the rune:

One Ring to rule them all, One Ring to find them,

One Ring to bring them all, and in the darkness bind them.

The darkness is near. Gandalf has already fought with Saruman the wizard, servant of Sauron. Frodo formally accepts the charge of the ring he carries, in succession to Bilbo. There are nine in the Fellowship: Gandalf, Aragorn, Boromir, Gimli the dwarf, Legolas, an Elf, and the four hobbits. And so the nine go out on their quest.

There is an immediate catastrophe: Gandalf falls in combat. Then comes a third interlude of consolation, the loveliest of all. It is in Lothlorien, the kingdom of the Elvenfolk and their Lord and Lady, Celeborn and Galadriel. In her presence the hobbits know a delight which becomes pure ecstasy. "I feel as if I were inside a song, if you take my meaning," says Sam. For him, as for Frodo, there has come an awakening, a recovery. He has discovered reality, that inner life which is greater than outward appearance. Tolkien, like Lewis, is profoundly Christian in giving this revelation not only to the heroic but also to the ordinary down-to-earth, everyday kind of hobbit.

Frodo at this moment feels himself to be "in a timeless land that did not fade or change or fall into forgetfulness". "Timeless" is the key word. There is a foretaste of eternity. Frodo knows that the memory of this will endure. When he returns to his own country he will still "walk there upon the grass . . . in fair Lothlorien".

That land is, like Kilmeny's country, a place of peace and light, of unflawed beauty. "No blemish or sickness or deformity could be seen in anything that grew upon the earth. In the land of Lorien there was no stain." It is "a sinless world" like the land in Kilmeny's journey.

Here every sense is quickened. This is no place of dream and illusion like the Elfhame of the ballads. Frodo can smell the grass and the trees, and hear a subtle diversity of sound in the rustle of the leaves, the rippling of water and the song of birds. The elves do not live here in blissful ignorance or heartless indifference to the griefs and fears of the outer world, as fairies do in legends. They are aware of the darkness beyond their land of light, of the peril Frodo and his comrades must face and overthrow before they too come back to this paradise.

Frodo is given an extra sense of touch, rather like that which Curdie gained from plunging his hands into the fire. When he climbs a tree he can feel its texture and the life within. He delights in the wood, in "the living tree itself". This is another manifestation of the kinship between all living things which has somehow been broken. Frodo loves all creatures and all created things for themselves. His love is pure and unpossessive. He sees their essence and feels the common bond shared by all created things. This is like MacDonald's vision.

The Lady Galadriel leads Frodo and Sam into her garden. From the stream that runs through it she fills a basin, breathes on it and bids them look. In that clearness they see things that were, things that are and things that will be. Sam sees Frodo asleep under a dark cliff, and himself climbing a dark stair; he has a glimpse of his home in the Shire where someone is cutting down the trees and where bad things are being done. He longs to return, but Galadriel tells him he cannot go alone. He resolves to stay with his master. Frodo sees people and scenes from the drama in which he is to play a part. He sees a stormy sea, a tall ship with black sails, a blood-red sunset. There is a fortress, fire, smoke and darkness, and, in the darkness, an eye searching for him. Galadriel knows what he has seen. She too has a ring and, if she had Frodo's also, she would become powerful beyond measure. That power would be at first beneficent. But not for long. In humility and self-oblation the Lady overcomes the temptation to power and accepts the future she can see. Even though Frodo will overcome Sauron, she sees that Lorien will, in time, be diminished and swept away.

On departing, the fellows are given food for the journey. They take thin cakes of *lambas* (way-bread or *viaticum*), more strengthening than any of ordinary baking. These are to be eaten only in need, and then only a little piece. They all drink the parting cup together and Galadriel brings to each a gift. For Aragorn there is a sheath that will keep his sword from stain or breaking, and a brooch with a green stone, the colour of hope. For Boromir there is a golden belt, and, for Merry and Pippin, silver belts. To Legolas she gives a bow and a quiver of arrows. Gimli declares it has been gift enough to have seen her and heard her speak, and he crowns his gallantry by begging for a lock of her hair. To Sam the gardener, lover of trees and of earth, she gives a little box of earth from her orchard. Finally, to Frodo she gives a crystal phial holding a star in water from her own fountain. It will be a light for him in the darkness to come.

So they set forth, followed, although they do not know it, by Gollum, the old adversary of Bilbo. He spies upon them and plots the capture of the ring. The friends go on to bitter darkness and to horror. In a fit of madness Boromir fails them. He is mortally wounded, but before he dies he performs an act of contrition. The Fellowship is broken by one catastrophe after another. In the end only Sam is left to follow Frodo.

The second volume of the saga, *The Two Towers*[63], is like the *maestoso* movement in a symphony. It comes to a paradise in the end but Frodo and Sam are very near a sort of hell in the beginning, wandering in desolation and confronting evil almost beyond resistance. Merry and Pippin are, for a while, lost; they cannot endure what Sam must suffer.

"So that was the job I had to do," Sam reflects, "when I started to help Mr Frodo to the last step and to die with him." He, the homely hobbit gardener, feels himself change and become like "some creature of stone or steel".

For both Sam and Frodo the climax of peril and horror is also the climax of heroism. It is the triumph of the ordinary hobbit. The whole saga is an exaltation of what are normally homely folk. The Elven people are noble and lovely, Aragorn is a prince, Gandalf is wise and subtle; but it is plain Frodo who must carry the ring to its final destruction, that destruction which alone can break the power of Sauron, and Sam stays with him until the end.

In this second volume there is little happiness, little light. But for Merry and Pippin there is comfort when, free again, they come to the camp of Faramir, brother of Boromir. They are only little hobbits; they have suffered enough. They have been brave within their capacity. To them supper at the camp is a feast: with Frodo and Sam, they sit down to eat with clean hands, from plates, with knives and forks, feasting upon bread and meat and good red cheese, dried fruits and pale yellow wine.

But Frodo's way is like the dark night of the soul, and Sam also has a glimpse of it, of something beyond the horror felt by Bilbo long ago, with temptations stronger and more subtle. At the end, after the last struggle between Frodo and Gollum, it is Gollum who takes the ring to destruction, also destroying himself in strange self-immolation, without contrition and with no turning to good at the moment of death. Yet it is Gollum who, by thus destroying the ring, defeats the evil of Sauron and overthrows his power. This small evil creature, ineffectual against good, proves effectual against the immense evil that has been so near victory. We are left with this enigma, a variation of the *felix culpa.*

For all others who have in some way fought for good and resisted evil, there is purgation. For Frodo there is something more: he is both purified and exalted. As he lies asleep in the house of Elrond, safe but sorely wounded, Sam looks at him: "A light seemed to be shining faintly within. . . Frodo's face was peaceful . . . but it looked old, old and beautiful." Such a look is often seen upon the face of the dead, but Frodo is returning to life and to something more than his former self.

They can none of them be the same again, not even the cheerful youngsters, Merry and Pippin, after their homecoming to the Shire. These two have, perhaps, not so much changed as become their true selves, grown to their full height.

The third volume of the trilogy, *The Return of the King*[64], is a story of fulfilment and of the healing of wounds. Aragorn has the royal touch. The triumphant culmination is seen in the procession of the Elvenfolk, where Celeborn rides with

Galadriel, Elrond and Arwen, "even-star of her people", who is now betrothed to Aragorn.

"Frodo, when he saw her come glimmering in the evening, with stars on her brow and a sweet fragrance about her, was moved with great wonder, and he said to Gandalf: 'At last I understand why we have waited! This is the ending. Now, not day only shall be beloved, but night shall be beautiful and blessed, and all its fear pass away!'"

In the beginning God created darkness and light, night and day, and saw that both were good. This is apocalyptic, beyond the utmost grandeur in Norse myth or saga. The Christian splendour is in it; the air is paradisal. Galadriel on her white horse, herself robed in shimmering white shining with light, is kin to the Queen in George MacDonald's *Princess* books, and like her she is a figure of Our Lady.

The tree symbolism recurs at the end. Gandalf, revived, healed and with a serene wisdom beyond any he has had before, shows Aragorn his kingdom. "This is your realm," he tells him, "the heart of the greater realm that shall be. The Third Age is ended and the new age is begun."

Aragorn plants by the fountain in the courtyard of his palace a sapling from the tree of life. The evil trees have been destroyed. There have been many that were good, such as the Ents who came to the aid of Frodo and Sam, expiating the ill done by the Willow in the dark wood long ago. The Ents are great and strong and wise; they are mighty defenders. Now, with the planting of the sapling, comes redemption for all trees.

This is the final Consolation for all who have shared the adventure of the Rings and known the perils. We leave Aragorn and the Elves and return with the hobbits to the Shire. Bilbo does not go with them: his way is beyond hobbitry now. For Merry and Pippin there is no more to do. But Sam must be with Frodo in the last combat which awaits him, the combat in which Frodo finally and forever overcomes Sauron. Now, with Sam's help, he has cleansed the Shire and cleansed the world. Here is the eucatastrophe.

For Sam it is the completely happy ending. He finds the wife of his heart, has children, is happy ever after. But Frodo needs and desires more than earthly comfort, more than hobbit blessings. He has obeyed the summons and saved his people; now another compulsion lies upon him, one which leads not to darkness and danger but to a place beyond his knowledge and guessing.

William Morris brings his heroes and heroines safely and gladly home. Walter, in *The Wood Beyond the World,* is made King, with the Maid he has rescued as his Queen; Birdalone is happy with her knight; Atra, the lonely one, finds comfort with the wood-lady; Ralph returns with his Ursula from the well at the world's end to his own town of Upmeads, where they both enjoy great happiness and enduring youth until the end of their days, when they both die on the same day and are buried in one tomb.

George MacDonald's Anados and the hero of *Lilith* come back from their vision of Paradise to wait in peace until they are called again. Arthur sails to Avalon, whence he may come again as rescuer in our final need. The children in the Narniad, with all their friends, go to Aslan's country for ever.

Frodo, like Arthur, however, must set sail once more. For Sam this parting is a grief which must be accepted patiently: this time he knows he is not being called to follow his master. For Sam there is the happiness of home. Frodo must go on to find the joy which is beyond this. There is light about him as he goes.

"The sails were drawn up and the wind blew, and slowly the ship slipped away down the long, grey firth, and the light in the glass of Galadriel which Frodo bore glimmered and was lost." Frodo smells a sweet fragrance, hears a singing voice. "It seemed to him that the rain curtain turned all to silver glass and was rolled back, and he beheld white shores, and beyond them a far green country under a swift sunrise."

Chapter 15

CONTINUANCE

Modern Writers of Fairy-Tales

Today the sense of wonder is still alert. Tolkien's four elements of fairy-tale are apparent in a diversity of contemporary books, especially, perhaps, the element of Recovery, the awakening to the true aspect of things and to their essence and reality. Apparent also is the Escape—escape not into a dream world but into one even more perilous than the one we know, an escape into adventure and conflict, with, in the end, a happy return to full Consolation.

It may be said in passing that strength and realism are also frequently apparent in modern historical novels for children, now blessedly purged of gadzookery and false romanticism. Many are written with insight, bringing the reader a recovery of vision. Some extend in time to the borders between history and legend. In Rosemary Sutcliff's magnificent book, *Sword at Sunset*, Arthur, leader and defender of Britain, who has his place in poetry and fantasy, is presented in the first person with convincing realism. There are other fine tales of far distant times: Marion Campbell's *Lances and Longships;* Kevin Crossley Holland's *Havelok the Dane* and *The Sea Stranger*. There is a certain affinity between such historical novels and sheer fantasy.

Modern fantasy follows various paths. One old and well-loved theme is a return to the past through an old house which has held succeeding generations of a single family, a house haunted by a benign presence or by the actors in an old drama. One of the loveliest of such returns or hauntings is presented in Alison Uttley's *A Traveller in Time*[65], in which Penelope, staying at the old farmhouse, Thackers, which has been for generations in her mother's family, finds herself in the sixteenth-century kitchen among a company from the past. The housekeeper appears to recognise and accept her as her niece, and she is drawn into the old life of the house. The owners are

126

the Babingtons, and Mary, Queen of Scots, is spending part of her captivity there. The plot to rescue her is being hatched. Penelope sees the Queen. She meets Anthony Babington and watches him ride away with his brother. As she knows her history, she knows what is going to happen. But the knowledge she brings with her from her own time cannot be communicated. There is sadness, but it is a loving and gentle sadness, full of brave and selfless devotion. Penelope tries to warn the Queen, but her voice will not carry over the centuries.

The detail is exquisite, as vivid as in a miniature. Such realism is based on Alison Uttley's own memories. Her childhood home, of which she has written so well, stood opposite the real Thackers, and the Babingtons were spoken of in the neighbourhood as a family but lately gone from the place.

Irish domestic magic is continued by Meta Mayne Reid, who writes of children going back into history, often to the early days of Christianity when the Other People still had the freedom of the woods. Alexandra, or Sandy, McNeill in *Sandy and the Hollow Book*[66] meets Angus, who is of that race. He becomes her friend, and she guards this secret in the heart of her mind. It is a secret that will be with her wherever she goes, opening strange doors. In *With Angus in the Forest*[67], Angus proves his power and benevolence by helping her in a crisis. Sandy's father, a scholar and librarian, is in danger of being dismissed for having spent a great sum of money upon a rare illuminated manuscript, the masterpiece of Peadar the scribe and painter, which some say is a forgery. Sandy's distress gives her extra perception and power. Looking intently at one of the miniatures of the manuscript, she suddenly finds herself within the picture, along with a girl in blue who is fleeing from the Vikings. The period is 900, during one of the invasions of Ireland. Sandy shares the girl's peril until, in the forest, they meet Angus, who, with Peadar the scribe, protects them. Sandy watches Peadar as he finishes a miniature, adding his signature, *Petrus Pictor Est*, by marking those letters in the text which make up this statement. On her return to her own time and place, Sandy recalls the incident and shows her father this proof of the manuscript's true authorship. "It was the girl in blue who made me look," says Sandy—and so brought vindication and a happy ending.

When the McNeills go to stay at the old family house,

Rathcaple, Angus appears again, but is known only to Sandy. Remembering his kindness, she tosses a bunch of primroses through the door of the ancient rath or hill-fort which gives the place its name. This is lovely and gentle magic, something like that of Patricia Lynch although lacking her incomparable humour.

The children in these stories are always protected. It is not so in every fantasy. The past and its people can be good and friendly but they can also bring menace and danger. Lucy Boston shows both aspects in her sequence about the old house of Green Knowe.

In *The Children of Green Knowe*[68], Tolly comes, a lonely small boy, to spend Christmas with his great-grandmother, Mrs Oldknow, and they fall in love with each other at first sight. "What does one generation more or less matter?" Nothing at all between kindred souls. Indeed even two or three centuries do not matter.

In Tolly's room at the top of the house, a room like a ship, there are four beds and some very old toys. They belonged, Mrs Oldknow tells him, to children who lived there three hundred years ago, and who sometimes return. They are Linnet, Toby and Alexander, and very soon they do come back.

They adopt Tolly, who is as blissfully happy with them as he is with Mrs Oldknow. The house itself is friendly too, but there is danger in the form of the demon-tree, Green Noah, which holds a curse laid upon the place long ago by a vengeful gipsy. Opposed to this evil is the statue of St Christopher, strong and holy, standing above the river, carrying the Child. With his help, the children defeat Green Noah.

In *The Chimneys of Green Knowe*[69], Tolly meets his kinsfolk of a more recent past, the eighteenth century. There are the blind, gentle and valiant Susan, her ill-disposed brother and a devoted black boy. At the end of this adventure Tolly and Mrs Oldknow find the long-lost treasure which saves the house from utter poverty.

So far the danger has been exciting rather than terrifying. In the last story of the sequence, *An Enemy at Green Knowe*[70], there is positive evil which almost destroys Tolly and his friend Ping, a Chinese refugee (who also loves Mrs Oldknow dearly and calls her "Grand Mother", very formally). The witch Melanie comes, demanding an old book of spells which Mrs Oldknow refuses to surrender. The children recognise and resist the evil but at first they do not realise its terrible strength. The conflict is almost too much for them as it is at times for the reader. This problem recurs in other fantasies where primal evil is let loose against the valiant resistance of a child or children, creating an almost unbearable tension. Eventually Tolly and Ping discover that Melanie's real name is Melusine, and this gives them power over her. In the end she is abandoned, spurned by her demon-lord and left a thing of naught, empty and cast away. Happiness returns to Green Knowe. Tolly's father comes home from abroad and with him Ping's father, who was thought lost or dead. But the problem remains: how much can children endure?

In fantasy, time past may drift across time present, and not only in an old house. Travellers may return to an ancient road. The return may not be frightening; it may even be beneficial. In Penelope Lively's moral and diverting tale, *The Driftway*[71], we have an excellent illustration of a boy's recovery through fantasy.

Paul, a selfish and rather stupid child, has run away from home, dragging after him his reluctant little sister. The remarriage of his widowed father has left Paul unjustly resentful and jealous. The young stepmother is kind and good, as the little sister knows. It is to their grandmother that Paul is taking his sister. On the road, the Driftway, the old drove road from Banbury to Northampton, they are given a lift by Bill the carrier, a man of much wisdom. Characters begin to come up out of the past, appearing to Paul, each telling his story. There is a boy fleeing from the invading Norsemen centuries ago, and another escaping from Naseby. All have troubles. Each draws Paul, at first unwilling, into his life. Paul listens, and slowly he begins to understand and to sympathise, to realise that his own trouble is imaginary and selfish.

Old Bill understands what is happening to Paul. "Most living's just jogging along, isn't it?" he asks. "But sometime in everybody's life there's a time when a whole lot of living gets crammed into a few minutes, or an hour or so, and it may be good or bad, but it's brighter and sharper than all the rest put together."

For Paul there has been an awakening, a recovery of sight. People have, over the centuries, left messages on the Driftway for those who can pick them up, and he, to his great benefit, has been able to do this. "Think yourself lucky," says Bill (when Paul admits that the Driftway is "a place that gets messages,") "They're not there for everyone." He has, in the common and sound phrase, been "taken out of himself" to return to a better, more sensible and more unselfish self. The children come to their grandmother's cottage and word is sent to their father that they are safe. They will go home to a new family life unspoiled by jealousy.

The theme of recovery through fantasy is also found in William Mayne, who is equally at home in strange borderlands and in a cathedral school. *A Game of Dark*[72] is a story of awakening, even of purgation. A boy is at odds with his father. The tension is caused by the father being crippled, while the boy resists, even resents, any compassion. He takes refuge in a dream of remote time, where he is in the household of a king. The dream comes suddenly, without his volition, and proves almost a purgatory. The final Consolation is being reconciled with his father, accepting the hardness of life and being at peace with himself and hence with others as well.

In what is perhaps William Mayne's profoundest fantasy, *Earthfasts*[73], there is little need for purgation for the two boys, David and Keith, who find themselves on the borders of perilous lands. They are good boys and loyal comrades, brave, imaginative and compassionate. All these virtues are apparent when they meet a strange figure emerging from the mound in Kendale near their home. They hear a sound of drumming, "like the thudding of invisible cold flames". Both feel that they are "at the heart of cold hell" with "the whole world . . . being torn at their feet". From a deep hole in the mound a flame shines and out marches a drummer boy, beating his drum and holding a candle. Both the light and the sound are uncanny. The light is white and cold, and it burns without diminishing the candle. But the drummer is no mere phantom. He can feel and return a pinch, and he is hungry and glad of the food the kind boys presently bring him. Meanwhile he tells his tale.

His name is Nellie Jack John and he is from the neighbouring village of Askeleth. His name reveals, as David and Keith know, that his own name is John, his father's Jack and his grandmother's Nellie. He had gone, an hour ago it seemed to him, beneath the castle mound to discover the treasure hidden there, the treasure which, as Keith and David know, belonged to

King Arthur who is perhaps asleep within that mound. To enter the mound may mean a long absence from this world: Nellie Jack John has been away for two hundred years.

The two boys befriend him. When, after visiting his own village and being rejected, he decides to return underground, they give him food and David's bicycle lamp to light his way. The candle which he held before is left with David and is the source of strong magic—and of danger. Keith is afraid of the continuously burning cold flame, but David looks into it and sees strange things. And strange things begin to happen. Giants appear, who steal a cow and pigs. A great wild boar attacks some people in the market and is shot dead. The great Jingle Stones are seen to move. Up at Watson's Farm a boggart appears, scaring Mrs Watson and the cat but doing no real harm. He is a mischievous nuisance, but has no ill will. He accepts the food put out for him and does his best to sweep the floor and wash the new-laid eggs. Later, Mr Watson relates how he tried to rid himself of the creature, first by cursing, then, in more Christian fashion, by blessing: "I stood there and lifted up my hand and said: 'Christ and His angels, and God Himself and the Holy Ghost be upon you, and remove you from this place to do evil in another place where folks don't mind.' " The boggart does not remove himself, but after that he does try very hard to be helpful. And so he is accepted.

This is homely and comic magic, if somewhat inconvenient to the Watsons. The real danger attacks David through the cold-burning candle. The two boys are together by the mound when darkness swoops down like a storm. Keith faints, and when he comes to himself David has vanished. He is thought to be dead, although no body is left behind. His father, the doctor, thinks he has been struck by lightning; the schoolmaster goes further and declares that he has been "vapourised".

Keith bravely goes in search of his comrade. By the cold light of the candle he sees a host of men whom he knows to be out of time and place. Their leader is Arthur himself, a menacing figure. Keith understands that somehow strange forces have been awakened; a power has been released which were best left asleep. The drummer boy started it by removing the candle from its proper place, and now Keith must put the candle back. Nellie Jack John ignorantly "disturbed the time that slept and the King that slept with it and he woke what had been asleep

131

before"—things like the giants, the boar, the boggart and the standing stones.

Arthur takes Keith up before him on his horse. At an opening into the hill, Keith leaps down and runs off into the darkness, still carrying the candle. The King and his horsemen ride after him. Keith comes to a round table with an empty candle socket and as he runs towards it the candle begins to waver, its flame to grow warm. He leaps on to the table and thrusts the candle into the empty socket.

"You've come, have you? I thought you wouldn't be long," says David, who is there, unharmed. It is the perfect greeting between comrades. On their way out of the mound they meet the drummer boy carrying the bicycle lamp and all escape together. As they approach their house, they see a light in the study window, and the doctor, whose own fortitude has been heroic, receives David back as if from the dead. The father has a marvellous capacity for accepting people, and he now accepts Nellie Jack John. "You're here now. And there's folk that want you," adds David.

Among these folk are the Watsons. The drummer boy had been reared on a farm "and can do owt". He is completely at home with the Watsons and with the boggart who, now grown somnolent, lives under the floor, ready to knock back if anyone knocks a greeting but otherwise inactive—which is just as well because it always addled the eggs it handled when it tried to be helpful.

The theme of this story is intricate. It deals with time past and time present, with disappearance and rescue, with the breaking of a law which must then be expiated (even if broken in ignorance), with fear which must be overcome by courage and loyalty. Young David and Keith prove that they would have made admirable knights. And the story is full of the most delectable humour. The boggart is within bowing distance of Brogeen.

Loyalty is again a theme in Ray Bradbury's *The Hallowe'en Tree*[14], in which, on All Hallows Eve, a band of boys, setting out on a round of their village as "guisers", enter a world of magic far beyond their imagining.

At the House of Haunts they find a tree hung with pumpkin lanterns. There they meet a mysterious stranger, Caripace Clavicle Moundsheet, come to take them through time and space, into the country where "everything that Hallowe'en ever was is buried". It could have been a marvellous adventure—they realise that their guide is protective—but one of their number is missing: the best of them all, Pipkin, "the greatest boy who ever lived, the grandest boy who ever fell out of a tree . . . a cross-section of all the boys who ever ran, fell, got up and ran again." They learn that Pipkin is dangerously ill and in great pain.

They fly through the centuries, going back to ancient Egypt, to the kingdom of Osiris, to the Britain of the Druids in their grove of oaks, to Africa and to Mexico. They see witches ride on Walpurgisnacht, and see the gargoyles on the roof of Notre Dame come alive. And always they see Pipkin, but always they lose him again. Finally Mr Moundsheet tells them that he is at the point of death: they can save him if they will each give a year from his own life. This they do, gladly. Arriving home again, they run to Pipkin's house and hear of his having been taken to hospital for an operation for an acute appendicitis. All is well, however, and Pipkin is now recovering. Midnight has come and gone: it is All Hallows.

Back at the House of Haunts, one of the children calls out to Mr Moundsheet: "Will we ever stop being afraid of nights and death?"

The reply comes: "When you reach the stars, boy, yes, and live there forever, all the fears will go, and Death himself will die."

King Arthur appears again in the work of other modern authors. He is the central character in the work of T. H. White, who fuses history with legend, and realism and beauty with daft and exuberant humour. His memorable and unique trilogy includes *The Sword in the Stone*[15], *The Witch in the Wood*[16] and *The Ill-Made Knight*[17]. Kings and knights, warlocks and witches are brought entrancingly to life. Mary Stewart, also, has more than a touch of magic in her stories of Merlin, *The Crystal Cave*[18] and *The Hollow Hills*[19].

More than one hill country in Britain claims Arthur. Perhaps he lies within the Eildon Hills on the Borders. It was indeed on the Borders that the historic Arthur fought his last victorious battle, at Coit Celidon, the wood of Celidon. By one account, Merlin, last of the great wizards, survived that battle but was left witless. A poor, crazed vagrant, he wandered about Tweedside until the people, who feared, hated and mocked him, stoned him to death. His grave is by the Powsail Burn near Drumelzier Kirk.

But, of course, it is easier to believe that Merlin, like Arthur, lives on and may come again. In more than one fantasy he has indeed come. The good wizard Cadellin in Alan Garner's two tales, *The Weirdstone of Brisingamen*[80] and *The Moon of Gomrath*[81], is, if not Merlin himself, very close kin to him. He guards a cave of sleeping knights and horses at Alderley Edge in Cheshire. Two children, Colin and Susan, come to stay with their mother's old nurse, Bess, now married to the farmer, Gowther Massock, an excellent character of steadfast strength, wisdom and integrity. They are very soon drawn into peril. Susan wears a bracelet with a clear crystal drop, the charm of the weirdstone. It had belonged to Bess, having been passed down through many generations of her family, and was finally given by her to Susan's mother, and so to the child. The forces of evil, in the person of Selina Place, are determined to possess the charm. Selina, a powerful and malignant witch, is, in truth, the Morrigan, the Third Bane of Britain. She has formidable assistants—the Swarts and other evil creatures—and controlling them all is Nostrond, evil incarnate, who dwells in that realm of darkness, Ragnarok.

The children have, however, strong defenders: Cadellin, Gowther, the good and comic dwarf Feodyree (known to his friends as Wineskin or Squabnose) and the lovely Lady of the Lake, Angharad or Golden Hand, whose island is a place of peace, healing and renewal. The children are taken there. "No evil will threaten us. For one night we may lie at peace, and the Lady will watch over us."

Angharad is like the Lady Galadriel whom Frodo reveres, and like the queenly mother figures in George MacDonald. The children's defenders are not always loving: they fight for themselves and are detached, although heroic and beautiful. Such is the Elf Lord Atlendor in *The Moon of Gomrath* to whom Susan gives her bracelet as a defence. Hers is a selfless act, but it brings much danger. *The Weirdstone* ends in victory for Cadellin, who overcomes the Morrigan and drives her to Ragnarok, bringing "joy and many tears". It is almost the eucatastrophe, but not yet. The Morrigan will return.

In *The Moon of Gomrath* Colin and Susan are involved in even worse conflict. Here, indeed, as in Lucy Boston's *Enemy at*

Green Knowe, we are genuinely afraid for the children. The powers of evil are too great for them to encounter; they are a burden beyond their strength. The dividing line between this agony of apprehension and the thrill of terror which has, all the time, the fairy-tale reassurance within it, is a very narrow one. And therein lies one of the problems of contemporary fantasy for children.

Again it is Susan who is in the deadlier peril. She is thrown into an enchanted sleep from which she can be roused only by the herb Mothan, which releases the Old Magic, quickened, unwittingly, when Susan and Colin light the beacon fire on the eve of Gomrath. Susan sees the riding of the Wild Huntsmen, who are infinitely more terrifying (although on her side) than the Stag Man whom Kay met in the forest.

Finally Angharad comes, benign, protective and strong, returning the bracelet to Susan and giving her, besides, the horn of gold and ivory which, long ago, before the beginning of history, belonged to the hero Fionn. It is to be sounded in alarm only when all else has failed.

Once again comes the Morrigan (the shape-shifter, the Loki of Scandinavian mythology) in female form. As the moon waxes, she is at the height of her power. Only Susan can overcome her, and only by sounding the horn. This summons the Wild Hunt, and with them come the Nine Women, led by the Stag Man with great antlered head. "We ride, we ride," they call. Finally they overthrow the Morrigan, then sweep in triumph up into the sky. Susan is left free and safe, but in anguish, for she would have chosen to go with them. Colin, too, has heard their cry, and to him it was a music "so beautiful that he never found rest again". They ride gloriously "over the waves and beyond the isles, and the Old Magic is free for ever". The land is purged of evil. Colin and Susan have played their part: they are secure, yet forlorn. There should have been a third movement in this symphony, bringing the children into peace and fulfilment.

Instead of writing this, Alan Garner chose a theme from *The Mabinogion,* the old legend of Blodeuwedd, the bride made from flowers by Math and Gwydion for Lleu Llaw Gyffes. She brings tragedy through her faithlessness and is cursed by Gwydion, who changes her into an owl, never to appear by day and always to be at enmity with other birds. This old story is retold, but not with a tragic ending, in *The Owl Service*[82]. The modern setting is an old house in Wales belonging to Alison, who is there with her mother, step-father and step-brother, Roger. The house is run by Nancy, who lives there always with her husband Huw the gardener and son Gwyn. The owl service is an old dinner-set, and the trouble begins when Alison chooses to copy the design, thus arousing a magic which should have remained quiescent.

Huw is a descendant of Lleu Llaw Gyffes, lordly by inheritance but not asserting it. "We are not free," he tells Gwyn. "No lord is free." He knows that Blodeuwedd is still expiating her sin, and that Alison has interrupted that expiation. "She wants to be flowers, but you make her owls," he tells Alison.

He sees the pattern of the legend woven again. "There are three who suffer every time, for in them the power of the valley is contained," he says, "and through them the power is loosed." Those who have lived and suffered intensely cannot die. They haunt the place of their agony until their guilt is cleansed. In this re-enactment, tragedy is averted. Alison is released from the danger she has brought on herself by Roger, who is steadfast and pure, detached from the past and yet compassionate. Alison finds her room filled with fragrance, with the petals of broom, meadow-sweet and oak-blossom out of which Math and Gwydion had long ago formed Blodeuwedd.

The setting here is that of the legend itself. But in *Elidor*[83] Alan Garner presents a convergence of time past and time present, a mingling of loveliness and industrial squalor. In a derelict street in Manchester, by a church about to be demolished, four children, Helen, Roland, Nicholas and David, are drawn into the magic of Elidor.

They meet a blind fiddler; the church disappears; they come to a castle on a cliff and are told of the lost treasures of the kingdom—the chalice, the sword, the spear, the golden stone. They hear the song:

> Fair is the land for all time
> Beneath snowfall of flowers,
> Magic land and full of song,
> Green Isle of the shadow of the stars.

They find the four treasures and bring them back to their own world. There, like fairy gold, they are transformed: the chalice becomes a cracked cup, the sword a wooden sword, the spear a spike of railing and the gold a common stone. Yet the magic lasts, conflicting with the modern magic of electricity in the washing machine and the television set. They give up the treasures, throwing them into the ruined church. Once they have done this, they see a light shine and hear the song. They know that somehow by their acts deliverance has come to Elidor. The end is Consolation.

In *Red Shift* there is again the theme of convergence of time, at a point of crisis in a boy's life. But here the magic is not convincing. The spells end in a mutter, and in the reader's mind there is no suspension of unbelief.

A sequence of stories by Susan Cooper is ruled by Merlin. The first three episodes of the sequence are *Over Sea, Under Stone*[84], *The Dark is Rising*[85] and *Greenwitch*[86].

The first tale, *Over Sea, Under Stone*, is set in Cornwall, in the village of Trewissick, where Jane, Simon and Barnabas, or Barney, are on holiday with their Great-Uncle Merry. He is known to them as Gumerry, but to the world of learning as Professor Merriman Lyon. However, by the end of the adventure, he is revealed as Merlin. They are staying in the cottage of a retired sailor, Captain Toms, who does not appear in this episode but who plays a great part in *Greenwitch*.

The discovery in the attic of an ancient manuscript rolled up in a telescope case sets off the conflict between the forces of Light, represented by Great-Uncle Merry and the children, and the powerful forces of Dark in the persons of Hastings, the owner of a yacht, his assistants, the Withers (a brother and sister), and two of the villagers, Bill and Mrs Falk. The manuscript is the common object of desire, and the forces of Dark are relentless in their efforts to possess it. The children are in desperate peril, especially after they come "over sea, under stone" to the cave where they find more treasure: yet another manuscript, and a golden chalice with an indecipherable inscription.

The confrontation comes: the tall, dark figure of Hastings in his yacht faces Barney, who holds the chalice and the manuscripts. Uncle Merry is coming to the rescue in a speedboat, but Hastings is nearer. In fury and defiance, Barney throws the treasures to Uncle Merry. He catches the chalice, but the manuscripts fall into the sea. The one in the tube sinks; the other is scattered and lost.

"The whole world seemed to stop and centre round the towering, black-clad man and a small boy." Then Uncle Merry, holding up the chalice, calls out some words in a strange tongue. "The dark figure in the other boat seemed to shrink within himself," till he "looked only ridiculous". It was the ultimate defeat.

The yacht sails away. The children are safe and the chief treasure remains with them. The manuscripts may be lost but the chalice, the holy grail itself, is safe. Only Merriman-Merlin knows its full, mystic power. To the world of learning it appears simply a rare antiquarian treasure. The children are given credit for their part in finding it and presenting it to the British Museum. By now they know something of the power of the chalice, and begin to realise who Uncle Merry is.

In *The Dark is Rising*, the forces of evil are stronger than ever. The magic is ancient, going back far beyond even Arthur's day, back into the shadows of prehistory. The hero, Will Stanton, seventh child of a seventh child, is one of a large, cheerful and apparently ordinary village family. He has been called to be one of the defenders of the Light for he is among the Old Ones, the guardians. He is the last and youngest of them. Will's eleventh birthday is on Midwinter Day, and on its eve he is given an amulet, an iron circle quartered by crossed lines, to wear as a buckle on his belt. The giver is another of the Old Ones, a good man, Dawson the farmer. Will tells him that he has met a strange old tramp on his way to Dawson's farm.

"So the Walker is abroad," says Dawson. A storm is blowing up. "This night will be bad, and tomorrow will be beyond imagining."

On the morrow, his birthday, Will finds himself out of his own world, back centuries, standing outside a smithy. He is confronted by the Rider, a black-cloaked figure on a black horse. The attack has begun. Will comes, in his journey in remote time, to a great hall where he is welcomed by the Lady and by a man who seems dimly familiar, as if remembered from his own time. He speaks prophetic words and shows Will strange visions: a vision of stones on a hillside; a vision of a ship struck by lightning; a vision of a horseman with the face of a stag, the eyes of an owl, the ears of a wolf and the body of a horse.

It is now that Will is told of his destiny and duty as one of the Old Ones, one "as old as the land, older even than that". He must serve the Light, helping to overthrow the Dark, "and nothing in this world or out of it may stand in the way of that service".

Will must find and guard the signs of Light. Already he wears the sign of iron. Merlin prophesies:

> When the Dark is rising, six shall turn it back,
> Three from the circle, three from the track;
> Wood, bronze, iron; water, fire, stone;
> Five will return and one go alone.

Already the Dark has begun to attack, and Will nearly yields—not to terror but to the pleading of voices in which he thinks he hears that of his mother. But the voices are false and evil.

Merlin and Will go out into the wintry wood. It is time to return to their own world, where they will soon meet. "We of the circle are placed only loosely within Time," says Merlin. "All times co-exist, and the future can sometimes affect the past even though the past is a road that leads to the future." That is a key statement: a key not only to the mystery of this book but to many others which present the convergence of time.

Back home again, where he had not been missed, Will goes carol-singing with the villagers to the Manor, where they are received by Miss Greythorne and her butler, Merriman, whom Will recognises as the Lady and Merlin of centuries ago. The forces of Dark return in the person of a visitor to Will's house. He is an acquaintance of Will's father, who innocently bids him enter. "I can cross your threshold," the visitor tells Will. "Your father, in good faith, asked me to enter the door." It is the old law of faery: Other People may enter a house only if invited.

The attack grows fierce. The Walker comes again as agent of the Dark. The evil surrounds the church and the villagers take refuge in the church hall.

Will learns more and more of the ancient wisdom: there have always been the forces and agents of Dark; there have always been the Old Ones. Magic was always an element of the world. "Men lived in it and with it, as a fish lives in water."

The evil grows stronger. The village is overwhelmed with snow: it is like a time of siege. The treacherous Walker dies, but first repents and so dies in peace. Will finds, one by one, the other elemental circles he must wear and the farm hand George, another of the Old Ones, links them together with links of gold.

The Huntsmen come, led by that recurring figure, Herne the Hunter, and the Dark is, for a time, driven out. But it will return; the Rider will ride again.

The next act in the drama is played in Cornwall. In *Greenwitch* the three children, Jane, Simon and Barney are there and Will is brought to join them, apparently by chance but really by the command of Merriman-Merlin, who now receives him as a comrade and equal (somewhat to the jealousy of the other three children). A disaster has befallen. The chalice has been stolen. They must all help to find it.

This time the agent of evil is the dark artist who sits drawing a sinister picture and who steals a sketch of Barney's and so gains power over its maker. The boys have their encounters with evil, not without danger, but it is Jane who plays the leading part in the story. The women of the village invite her one night to their ritual making of the Greenwitch, a great figure with a frame of hazel branches, weighted inside with stones, and with hawthorn blossom for the body and rowan for the head. The fishermen will throw it into the sea: the Greenwitch is the scapegoat, bearing away the sins of the people; it is a bringer of luck, the image of a goddess. Jane, however, sees no "she-like quality" in the Greenwitch, which has, rather, the aspect and essence of a tree or a rock.

When the figure is finished, each of its makers may utter a wish. Jane is bidden by a stern but kind woman to speak hers and she is suddenly filled with compassion for the great, lonely image. "I wish you could be happy," she says to the Greenwitch.

"A perilous wish," says the stern, kind woman, "but good may come of it." And indeed it does.

The three children and the three Old Ones, Merriman, Will and Captain Toms, are caught up in the conflict with the Dark. The dark artist, the boys discover, has the chalice hidden in his caravan, where Barney is, for a time, spellbound. He speaks in a strange voice of "the spell of Mana and the spell of Reck and the spell of Lir", all powerful spells, yet all of no avail "if Tethys has a mind against you". It is the old sea magic, with the old Celtic gods. Tethys, goddess of the sea in long distant ages, is more powerful than any other.

Jane dreams of the Greenwitch under the sea, holding what looks like the telescope tube which contained the lost manuscript. But the tube shines like gold.

The climax comes: the three Old Ones attack the Dark while the three children are protected by merciful oblivion. Will and Merriman-Merlin plunge into the depths of the sea. They have recovered Barney's drawing and they take this as a gift to Tethys. In return, the goddess permits the Greenwitch to give them the treasure she holds. The Greenwitch is willing, for she remembers Jane's wish, the first selfless, compassionate wish uttered upon her through the centuries.

The Dark is defeated and its agent, the dark artist, is left helpless. The chalice is found and its rune can now be deciphered through a clue given in the recovered manuscript. The three Old Ones read it, and then crumble the manuscript to powder.

In a final enchantment, the dark artist is carried away by the forces of Wild Magic, and life becomes serene again. Will fashions a strip of gold engraved with the words: "Power from the Greenwitch lost beneath the sea." This Jane throws to the Greenwitch in the sea. That night she has a good dream, and wakens to find her room strewn with leaves, hawthorn blossom and rowan, all fresh with the scent of the sea.

Celtic and Druidic magic is very strong and perilous. That old world where the new Christian faith came to meet the ancient is the scene of two marvellous books by Winifred Finlay, *The Singing Stones*[87] and *Beadbonny Ash*[88]. In the former, Christie's imagination, inherited from Celtic or Pictish forebears, is tinged with a second sight that is not altogether comfortable. She has acquired two green stones, both engraved with the design of a little beast with a curly tail in place of feet, and a long snout. One of these, bought in Edinburgh from a shop in the Royal Mile, is the source of all her adventures, which are shared by her brother Ian and his friend Peter. From the stones comes singing and a vision. The owner of the shop pursues Christie with a menace she feels to be more than human, a feeling justified by later events.

The three children are staying with Christie and Ian's grandmother in Perthshire, a region with many old Pictish memories. Gran is a character of strength and no nonsense, but some of her friends, most estimable ladies, are aware of much more than is apparent in everyday life. A young man, Alastair, an assistant in the shop where Christie bought the stone, comes to camp in the neighbourhood. He is an amiable youth, but weak and subservient to his employer, who returns once more, threatening. The danger increases as the mystery becomes clearer.

On the great stone of Dunfallany, carved centuries ago by the Pictish artist Talorcan, Christie sees once more the design of the little beast, and sees two such creatures themselves, come alive, out of the water. They are the *each uisge,* the water horses. The singing of Christie's magic stones has brought them out of the past. They are friendly beasties, unlike the *each uisge* of many legends, and talk to Christie about the coming of St Columba who brought the Gospel to Pictland. He dealt very gently with all the creatures he met, offering them the choice of either staying as they were or entering the service of the Lord who died upon the cross for all creation. The People of Peace, the *Sidhe,* and others had chosen not to change. But they had all departed long ago. Only the two little water horses could still return over the centuries. Talorcan used to ride on them about the country, carving his stones and crosses. He was good, but not strong enough in faith to resist the enchanter Loki, the shape-shifter, enemy of all good, who now had come back in the shape of the menacing stranger. He knows, though Christie until now did not know it, that in the past she was the Maiden, his adversary, who may now overcome and banish him.

So, the conflict begins. The boys are drawn into it and, as often in fairy-tale, there is a faithful animal, Gran's dog Dougall, of a very mixed breed but unflawed courage and loyalty. In the end, after a desperate struggle, Loki is defeated and Talorcan revived. Christie is shown his masterpiece, the carved Stone of Destiny, hidden from the English by the monks who sank it deep in a bog.

Back in the present time, there is a night of storm, of thunder and hail and freezing cold. Alastair in his tent is struck senseless, almost lifeless. His master rescues him and, in restoring him to life, himself dies. By that selfless act he, Loki, is purged of all his evil and set free.

Christie is a good child, loyal, brave and loving, and strong enough for the perilous task to which she has been called. In *Beadbonny Ash*, Bridie goes wilfully into a past more terrible than she could imagine, and draws others with her into danger and near death. Christie is the child of loving, devoted and sympathetic parents, who help her in the conflict. Bridie is the child of a broken marriage. Her father was killed in a motor accident when she was with him, and she is antagonistic to her mother. She has taken refuge in self-centred fantasies. From such delusions it is all too easy to pass into "the perilous realms".

It all happens in Mull, where Bridie is staying with her mother's old friend, kind Mary Macdonald, her husband and three children—John, a medical student, Sheena, who is gentle and quiet, and Kenneth, who rarely stops talking. There is also Calum, a local character of considerable force, eccentricity and fun.

The "beadbonny ash" (the phrase is quoted from a poem by Gerard Manley Hopkins) is the rowan tree which grows by the door of the house in Mull. It is the holy tree which guards the threshold from unwelcome entrants and keeps from harm any who wear a spray of those "beadbonny" berries, as red as the holy blood. Calum has given a spray of them to Sheena.

The past into which the four children are drawn, and Calum after them, is on that dim borderland between the ancient and the new faith. Bridie is a princess, daughter of a goddess mother, but she is not free. Against her stands the high priest Broichan with his attendant, the malignant dwarf. The setting is a culmination of all Bridie's dreams and fantasies, and yet she is unhappy. Her mother, goddess of birth and death, who cares for women in labour and for the dying, is coming to the end of her powers for Columba is turning people to the new faith. She is stern with her daughter, rebuking her for lack of love, as Calum also rebukes her. "In your selfishness and ignorance you are meddling in the old arts," she is told, "and now it is disaster you are bringing"—a disaster brought upon her people in the past and upon those she has drawn with her from the present, especially upon the gentle and innocent Sheena, who is taken captive. Calum rescues her, Calum who in their own time gave her the protective rowan, Calum the local character, who deliberately cultivated and presented his eccentricity and who was regarded by the contemptuous Bridie as an ill-washed, disreputable misfit. In the old world he is heroic, steadfast and wise—his true self. Bridie realises this, and sees also the immense loneliness of her mother, sees, at last, with contrition, her own selfishness.

"Give me time," she pleads. "I am full of love, but I have wasted it on dreams and make-believe." It is the moment of truth, the beginning of recovery. In some of the old legends the wanderer into Elfhame suddenly realises the hollowness and the ugliness of things that before had seemed of alluring glamour. Bridie comes to that same realisation.

Her conversion brings about that of her mother, who now appears radiant, benign and humble, hailing the coming of the Son of Mary and Mary herself, Mother and Queen. Bridie bears the name of St Bridget, Bride of the Isles, who according to a lovely tradition was taken to Bethlehem to be nurse to Mary in her child-bearing, and to the Holy Child.

The evil has passed, but not the danger. There is a great storm. A wave breaks over the boat in which Calum is rowing the children back to their own place and time. Sheena is swept into the sea and Calum leaps after her. Darkness overwhelms them. Bridie wakens in the cottage in Mull, ill but safe. Her mother is with her—the mother whom she, in her selfish folly, had come near to hating. There is a loving reconciliation. The other children are safe too—but Calum has been drowned.

The four young people remember their journey back in time, the people they met and the perils they suffered. Sheena still carries the sprig of rowan. She tells Bridie about a young man from Iona who appeared to rescue them, but no such man can be found, no-one has seen him. Kenneth declares that it must have been Columba himself, come through the centuries to save them.

But Calum is dead, and Bridie is broken-hearted, feeling it to be by her fault. Sheena comforts her. Calum had one great love: the sea. Now the sea has taken him in the death he would have chosen. Kenneth adds his consolation: Calum is already a hero and he will soon become a legend. "Another couple of years and he'll be a folk-hero, and there'll be bearded blokes with tape-recorders collecting stories about him." Which, to Calum, would be ecstasy.

Celtic and northern magic is full of the sea. There are legends of seals, those enchanted children of a king, according to one tradition, who are close to humankind, changing often into human form, yet never forgetting their home under the waves.

144

Rosemary Harris, in *The Seal Singing*[89], has hints and reminders of this magic. Her children have a deep love of the seals, deeper than their affection for any other creature. They are the Carrigans, Catriona and Toby, living on their island of Carrigona in the Hebrides.

Toby has a special affection for the baby seal, Plushet. They know the tradition that seals will respond to the singing of the right singer. The picture of the children's life on the island is almost idyllic, none the less so for being a salty mixture of realism and comedy, with much of the latter being provided by Calum, very much a man of Glasgow, and housekeeper Anny, who stands no nonsense.

The arrival of a cousin, Miranda, a wilful and over-sophisticated girl, shatters the happiness and security. Miranda is tainted by vanity, cruelty and treachery. There seems to be something in her of their ancestress Lucy, whose name is shadowed, though what mischief she did and what punishment she suffered, they do not know. Lucy used to sing to the seals, drawing them up to the shore to listen to her singing. Did she at one time harm them, as Miranda seems about to do now?

But this second tragedy is averted. The baby seal, Plushet, is shot, but it recovers. Miranda is cleansed of her fault and, in part through this, Lucy fulfils her expiation. This is a fantasy of contrition, recovery and consolation. Human bones—almost certainly those of Lucy—are discovered in unconsecrated ground and are given Christian burial in the old chapel by the shore, a chapel dedicated to St Culzean, patron saint of the family and protector of seals. Lucy's restless spirit is now absolved and at peace, and the seals return to the island.

The love between a man and a seal-woman, or a woman and a seal-man, has often been told. Ronald Lockley's *Seal Woman*[90] is an Irish girl named Shian, said to have been found, a new-born baby, in a seal cave. She herself believes this, believes herself to be a sea-princess, and she shuns human ways and domestic life. Wild and alluring, she binds with a spell the narrator of the book, an Englishman, who discovers her and returns to the lonely south-west coast of Ireland, to a hidden place, Kilcalla. Shian draws him into the kingdom of the seals. At intervals he returns to his former life in London, but for him reality is in those western seas and caves.

145

In Hans Andersen's story of the Little Mermaid, the sea-maiden would give anything to be with her beloved human Prince who has forsaken her for a human bride. But in the seal legends the sea holds its children and continually lures them back.

Seal Woman is almost too sad and haunting for children. It must be read with a total submission, with a complete suspension of unbelief, an immersion, as it were, in the sea of enchantment. Shian bears her lover a daughter and herself vanishes. He brings the child to his sister to be reared and he has written the tale for her. He will not take her back to her birthplace.

George Mackay Brown, the Orcadian poet and magic-maker, has written two tales[91] of the love between a woman and a seal-man—good tales of happiness for the woman. *The Vanishing Islands* tells of a young man from the Orkneys in a sealskin coat who speaks to a girl cutting peats on the island of Rousay, asking her to come with him. She goes, and is never seen again in Rousay. But years later her father and brothers, out fishing, are lost in a fog and come thankfully to an island where they see a fine house. The woman of the house welcomes them and gives them a drink in scallop shells, a drink such as they have never tasted, "as if all the precious, succulent things of the sea had been made to yield their essence: pearl and seaweed and mussel." But the old father does not drink. He can only look at the woman, at the two children playing with shells by the fire and at the baby in the cradle. He is sad and the woman speaks gently to him. He tells her of the heartbreak that came to his wife and him twenty years before when their daughter disappeared.

The woman's husband comes in, a tall man in a sealskin coat, followed by two tall sons each with a good catch of fish. The woman offers some to her guests to take home, but the old man refuses. It is she he wants, his lost daughter. Let her leave her *selkie-men* and live again among her own folk and die a Christian death. But she will not go. Her place is here with her husband and their children. "I have lived here too long," she says. "The taste of corn in my mouth would kill me."

In George Mackay Brown's other story, *The Seal King*, a knight, Odivere, of no great nobility of character, wins by black magic a lovely bride who has not at all wanted to be married. She

146

proves a good wife, but she is unhappy. She has no child and she has lost her freedom. Her only joy is walking by the shore, watching the coming of the seals and whistling to them, for they love her tunes.

One day Odivere goes off to the Crusades, leaving his wife a golden necklace as a love token. In her loneliness she goes more and more to the coast to sing to the seals. One day a great bull seal swims to shore. The lady runs up to the herd-road and, looking back, sees that where the seal landed a man now stands with his hand raised in greeting.

Six years pass with no news of Odivere. Then one day a knight comes bearing news. His voice sounds "like the muted thunder of a western sea, like cliff-cries and cave-echoes". The news, although he tells it gently, is not good. Odivere is well—better, perhaps, than a brave Crusader should be—but he is earning a name for himself as a gambler and as a lover, rather than as a warrior and defender of the Christian faith.

Night falls darkly, and the lady bids her guest stay. He tells her they have met years before, down on the shore. But she had run away.

In the morning the strange knight departs. Next winter a boy is born to a young fisherman and his wife, much to the surprise of everyone, for the woman had shown no signs of pregnancy. He is a beautiful boy, quite unlike his parents, who, though they were poor folk, now seem to have all kinds of luxuries. The lady of the castle takes a great and tender interest in the child, giving him a precious gift, a fine gold chain.

Then one day the child disappears. He is last seen in the sea, watching a herd of seals. His body is never found, only his little shirt and breeches. The fisherman and his wife are stricken, but the Lady is serene.

The next event is the homecoming, at last, of Odivere. This is celebrated with feasting, followed by an otter-hunt, when, down on the shore, he brings ill luck by killing a young seal. Round its neck is a golden chain, Odivere's love-gift to his wife, long ago.

"You have killed my son," his wife tells him.

In a jealous rage he has her tried for adultery. She makes no defence: the charge is proven. When a servant takes the body of the young seal to be buried, the sealskin comes off and he finds himself holding the body of a child. He tells the priest of this, and the boy is given a Christian burial. The Lady is doomed to be burned, but on the morning of the execution a school of whales appears and Odivere orders a hunt. No whale is killed, however. They all swim away, and the men return to the castle for the burning.

"We earth-dwellers will never know the huge sympathy that binds together the creatures of the sea, so that when a terrible wrong has been committed, a single pulse of pity beats through the cold, world-girdling element, and seal, pearl, whale and sea-blossom devise with their God-given instincts that which will restore beauty and wholeness to the breached web."

While the men are hunting the whales, the seals come swimming ashore, standing among the rocks as men. They come up to the castle where the lady lies bound and, taking the chains from her, they carry her down to the shore and into the sea, to the kingdom of the seal King—her faithful lover.

This is the purest distillation of sea magic given us in our time. It has the enchantment, the sadness and the wonder of Hans Andersen's most haunting tales, the quality of northernness of which C.S. Lewis has written. It is a sea-song, a sea-blossom, a pearl.

Such tales of sea and island magic have authentic settings. They happen in real places; they are part of realistic, credible folk-lore. In Ursula Le Guin's trilogy, *Wizard of Earthsea*[92], *The Tombs of Atuan*[93] and *The Farthest Shore*[94], the sea magic has become myth. We are transported into a new realm, a new dimension where magic is part of daily life. Her characters are human but remote in time and space, out of this world. *Wizard of Earthsea* introduces the hero, Sparrowhawk, born in Gont, an island in a vast archipelago. Destined to be a wizard, he is taught the rudiments of enchantment by his aunt (rather as Fionn, the Irish hero, was trained by two Wise Women), then by a good wizard, Ogion. He is then ready to go to the School of Wizards on the island of Roke.

It is a fantastic, unearthly tale, yet it has realism. Its world resembles our world, but it is our world transmuted by magic. Once this difference is accepted, the similarity is clear. The wizards' school has much in common with any school and the pupils or apprentices are human and varied. Young Sparrowhawk is soon deep in strange studies. He learns mastery over winds and weather, the properties of herbs, the art of illusion and the Old Speech in which all magic is uttered, much as a grammar or public school boy in this ordinary world of ours learns history, mathematics and the classics. Like any schoolboy, Sparrowhawk also learns to make friends, to accept discipline, to conform. Later he progresses to higher studies as another boy might go to college and read for a degree.

Sparrowhawk is clearly capable of wisdom and heroism, but he sins through pride. He summons a spirit of darkness so powerful that it almost destroys him. He is saved by the Archmage, the chief wizard Nemmerle, but Nemmerle dies in the conflict. Sparrowhawk is left with a shadow that will long haunt him. One is reminded of the shadow which follows Anados in *Phantastes*. The new Archmage tells him that he has released a spirit of *un-life*. "The power you had to call it gives it power over you," he is told. "It is the shadow of your arrogance, your ignorance."

Sparrowhawk, duly trained as a Master in Wizardry, goes as resident sorcerer to a small island in the archipelago. Now comes his first great test. He must defeat a dragon: a foe, but a glorious foe. The very danger is splendid. The shadow still haunts him, "that formless, hopeless horror... a creature of a lightless, placeless, timeless realm". To atone for his sin, Sparrowhawk must make a long, purgatorial expiation, and this is the theme of this book. This fantasy contains Tolkien's essential elements: Recovery, Escape and Consolation.

The sequel, *The Tombs of Atuan*, is chiefly the story of the girl Arha. Destined to be high priestess, she is trained in the Tombs. This is the realm of matriarchal rule and magic. To this place of caves and labyrinths no man may be admitted. If one does enter, he must die. And one man has come, and awaits death in the darkest depths of the caves. There Arha finds him. It is Sparrowhawk, much progressed in power and knowledge and now bearing his true name of Ged. He has with him a precious amulet, half of the ring once worn by the greatest of all wizard kings, Ereth-akbe. Arha has learned of this king, of his valour and his defeat, of the breaking of his staff and of his ring. The other half of the ring lies hidden in the Tombs.

The tale tells how Arha, in compassion and with infinite danger to herself, helps Ged to find the other half of the broken ring and to escape, through dreadful darkness, to the sea. There they find Ged's boat and sail in safety to the city of Havnor. For Arha, Havnor is her refuge and home, and her tale ends there.

The tale of Ged is contined in *The Farthest Shore,* He has returned to Roke as Archmage, and there he receives the young Prince, Arren of Enlad, come to implore help against the evil that is creeping up on his father's kingdom and on all the islands of the archipelago. The old magic is threatened.

Ged and Arren set forth together on the most perilous voyage of all. In the midst of the danger there is a lovely interlude among the happy colony of Sea Folk who live on rafts. But terror returns, mounting to a climax of almost unbearable fear and horror, bringing the loss of all faith and security. For the Prince it is a purgatory very close to Hell. Even Ged is tried to the limits of his strength.

A great dragon appears, speaking to Ged in the Old Speech, summoning him further. This is the great Orm Embar, descendant of the mightiest dragon of all, Kalessin. Since his battle with them, long ago in his youth, Ged has won the friendship of the dragons.

Ged's last journey is to the farthest shore, the realm of death. He encounters the Dark Master in a conflict in which he and the Prince are nearly killed. In the Dry Land of utter desolation, Ged and Arren meet Cob, a blind, ghastly and ghostly figure, long dead, who has re-made himself.

Ged tells him that he is utter emptiness: "You have no self... You have given everything for nothing." Ged compels Cob to take them to the last place of all, the source of the Dry River, the half-shut door between two worlds, beyond which lies neither light nor darkness, life nor death. Ged speaks one word of power, then says: "Be thou made whole." He draws a rune upon the half-shut door, which finally closes. Then he speaks again: "By the word that will not be spoken until time's end, I summoned thee. By the word that was spoken at the making of things I now release thee." It is the final exorcism. Cob departs forever.

It is the final victory in the battle for which Ged has been trained and prepared since boyhood, and it has brought him very near death. He told the young Prince on one stage of their journey: "Only that is ours which we are willing to lose. That selfhood, our torment and our glory, our humanity does not endure." There is an echo in this of holier words.

Arren tries to carry Ged, now drained of life. But where can he take him? There is no refuge. Helpless and hopeless, he finds in his pocket a little black stone, picked up on their wanderings: a fragment from the Mountains of Pain. Holding it he knows "alone and unpraised and at the end of the world, Victory". He has come through his purgatory.

Consolation follows Recovery. The great dragon, the greatest of all, Kalessin, swoops down and bids Arren and Ged to mount him, with Ged in his arms. There is "the morning of the world" in his eyes as he looks at the Prince, and a "profound and mild hilarity". Before he departs Kalessin bears Ged and the young Prince back to Roke, to security, comfort and home. "He has done with doing," says the wise door-keeper. "He has gone home."

Ged, too, has "done with doing". He attends the coronation of Arren as King in Havnor, then goes down to the shore where his boat Lookfast is lying, and departs therein without wind or sail or oar. Like Frodo, he has gone beyond telling, beyond knowledge. The end is good.

This trilogy, like *Lord of the Rings*, has invented a new geography and a new mythology. The wizards are still human, but with a power and wisdom beyond human scope, acquired under discipline, like any human skill and scholarship.

Wizard of Earthsea, the account of young Sparrowhawk's progress, failure, atonement, rivalries and friendships, has comedy and warmth. The magic becomes more remote, more terrible, in *The Tombs of Atuan*, and the danger mounts in *The Farthest Shore*. But then comes kindliness again, with gentleness, loyalty and endurance to the end.

This trilogy is, as a whole, nearer to Tolkien's divine comedy than to any contemporary fantasy, but it lacks the unique homeliness and good earthiness of hobbitry—the virtue so stressed by the American critic, William Ready[95], in his *Understanding Tolkien and "The Lord of the Rings"*. He writes there of Frodo as "a little hobbit . . . who is man in essence", and more than a man, as Bilbo is although Bilbo is a poet who discovers himself and his vocation only after his adventure. *The Lord of the Rings* is set in strange lands,

151

sometimes in the most perilous of realms, but it begins in the homely, comfortable Shire of the hobbits.

"The whole core of Tolkien's work is man-centred," writes Ready, "and spiritual thereby." This is a profoundly Christian statement which would have delighted the spiritual progenitor of so many makers of myth, George MacDonald. And it is by this balance or blending of the human and the spiritual that we may judge both the old and the new fantasies.

Chapter 16

THE SUMMING UP

Fairy-Tale in the Post-War World

The background to the nineteenth-century tales of myth and magic was, for those above a certain social level, one of apparent stability, comfort and order, at both the domestic and the national level. But there was another aspect to Victorian Britain. Disraeli had written about "the two nations", split by a deep social divison, and George MacDonald, too, was aware of injustice, of the depth of human misery and of the greed and cruelty that lay beneath contemporary life like the goblins beneath the castle.

A knowlede of poverty is apparent also in E. Nesbit's account of lame little Dickie Harding, although of sheer cruelty and misery she did not speak. Her Edwardian world was not far removed from the Victorian, although comfort and ease had increased over a wider range of the middle class.

There was a sudden change with the First World War, but after it there was a repairing of the surface of civilised life. There was still security in the magic as well as in the domestic world. Looking back to the 'twenties and 'thirties, the older generation may see those decades almost as a world of illusion. There was still a clear dividing line between comfort and poverty, security and unemployment, which could bring despair. However, for those on the safe side it was a pleasant world—for all but the far-sighted who could see that beyond the shadow of poverty lay the darker shadow of war. Presently that shadow took shape and became reality.

The Narnian tales and *The Lord of the Rings* appeared soon after the second world war, when evil had come very close to victory. There has been little diminishing of this realisation in the last thirty years, and there is a corresponding awareness, in books for children and among the children themselves, of something deeper than the poverty and degradation recognised by good and compassionate Victorians.

Myth-making continues. The renaissance of wonder has reached maturity. And we need it. The conflict between good and evil—absolute evil—in which the child heroes of fantasy are caught up and taxed to the limit of their endurance has become a common theme. But there is still beauty, still gentleness, and there is still the revelation of kinship between all living things. And time has brought so many changes that the journey into the past can be made over less than a century.

In Philippa Pearce's gentle story, *Tom's Midnight Garden*[96], there is not even a *revenante* from the past. Tom, staying with his aunt and uncle in a block of flats which had once been one large house, enters the lost garden at midnight and meets a friendly little girl. He meets her more than once, and finds that after each visit she has grown older, till soon she reaches young womanhood. On the last day of his visit, Tom discovers that she is still alive in real life, but an old woman now. She lives in one of the flats in what was once her parents' house. The years between are no barrier: the old lady and the boy recognise each other. Their friendship has been no dream. They know how to talk to each other. Both are innocent of selfish and possessive affection.

So, too, is Carrie in Helen Cresswell's *Up the Pier*[97]. Here a family return from the recent past (remote enough to Carrie) of the 1920's. A selfish old man would compel them to stay, holding them in the present against their will, but Carrie has the power and the selflessness to release them, sending them back to their own time.

There are other worlds within or beyond ours, like that into which Joy Chant almost hurls her children in *Red Moon and Black Mountain*[98]. Here a boy playing his pipe compels Oliver to enter Kedrinn, the Starlit Land, where he is welcomed in the name of the High King and trained to be leader of the young warriors. He must fight and overthrow the dark enchanter. But even then his task is not ended. He must enter a cave and meet the Priestess and must offer himself to the Goddess. Again it is the ancient, matriarchal world of magic. Oliver's younger sister and brother, Penelope and Nicholas, are drawn into this world too, and into the perilous service of the lovely Star Princess. Their adventure is bearable and credible, but Oliver's is over-burdened with terror. There are moments, too, when disbelief breaks in and insists that this is merely the dream-world of a boy, for every boy sees himself as warrior, leader and hero. Yet the story has depth, has Fantasy, Recovery and Consolation. Oliver returns to our common, warm and welcoming world and finds Penelope and Nicholas safe. He sees again the boy in the tree, playing his pipe. The boy offers Oliver water to drink, which cleanses and heals him.

"I am the Lord of Wood and Water," says the boy. "I am the Leader of the Great Dance. I am the guide, I am the messenger, I am the Reborn, the Young King, the spring and summer... the Lord of life and laughter."

He offers Oliver the wine of oblivion, but Oliver refuses it. He has come through his ordeal; he has lost innocence. But, as the piper tells him, "Virtue lies not in ignorance of evil but in resistance to it." So Oliver chooses to remember. He has reached maturity.

There is primal evil here as well as primitive worship. The enemy is the oldest of all: the fallen angel "made to be a mighty servant. . . . still a mighty foe." "He cannot make, he can only corrupt."

The goddess figure appears again in Joan Aiken's tale of sea magic, presented as a play, *Winterthing*[99]. Her earlier enchantments were of lighter sort, well mixed with comedy and sometimes agreeably spiced with melodrama. Such are a quantity of her short stories including *A Small Pinch of Weather, All You Ever Wanted* and *A Necklace of Raindrops*, and so too are her hilarious mock-histories of a nineteenth-century England which is not Victorian because the Stewarts have been restored in the amiable person of King James the Third. These begin with *The Wolves of Willoughby Chase*[100], in which the witch-governess makes her first appearance, continue with *Black Hearts in Battersea*[101] and its sequels, and include the Welsh magic of *The Whispering Mountain*[102]. No other writer of fantasy has given us this blend of history, both social and domestic (the account of nineteenth-century London is as realistic as any Victorian story of poor children), exuberant humour, melodrama and magic, all recounted in the most matter-of-fact way.

In *Winterthing*, however, there are new qualities: sheer beauty and poetry, and deep compassion. Four children, Rendal, Lem, Jakin and Carilan, come to Winter Island in the Hebrides with "Auntie". She is no relation to them; neither are

155

they related to each other. She, a kleptomaniac and sadly aware of it, has stolen them, one by one, in babyhood, and has brought them to this remote place so that she can escape the temptation of shops and the probable penalty of a mental hospital.

They are brought over from the mainland by a ferrywoman, Mrs Macrae, who warns them that Winter Island is an enchanted outpost between summer and winter; that every seventh year it disappears all winter, only to reappear in spring. Rendal, the elder girl and a wise child, finds that they cannot pay the ferrywoman because she cannot find Auntie's purse. Mrs Macrae says she will return for payment. Both the purse and Auntie's note-book have been stolen by Carilan, a bad and corrupt child. Having thus discovered the name and address of her own parents, she burns the book.

Auntie, wandering about the island, finds and lovingly adopts a lost baby, whom she calls Sedna. Carilan is bitterly jealous and reacts with cruelty. Rendal and Lem are kind: they feed the child and sing to her. Sedna grows extraordinarily rapidly. Always she wears an old shawl, until vicious Carilan burns it. Out of this fire Sedna, grown out of babyhood within a day or so, plucks a black shawl which makes her invisible.

Carilan escapes with a stranger, an outlaw wanted by the police, whose boat is driven ashore. She intends to go in search of her parents. In a sudden violent storm the boat, with the stranger and Carilan in it, is sunk. Jakin, who is not cruel as she is but who is altogether selfish, also plans his escape. A great frost falls upon land and sea and Jakin sets off to walk across the ice, but it breaks and he too is drowned. It is the old, stern morality of fairy-tale: the bad of heart must die. The kind and compassionate are safe, the helpless protected.

The child Sedna disappears. The ferrywoman comes back, not to ask for payment but to tell Rendal benignly that she has been paid over and over again with kindness from these three who remain, for it was she who took the form of the lost child Sedna, so well cherished by Auntie, Rendal and Lem. She reveals herself as a sea-goddess, strong and protective. All will go well in the enchanted hidden winter which is to come. Auntie will sleep; Rendal and Lem will be attended by the servants of the goddess, the elements. These elements have destroyed Carilan and Jakin, but it was the evil nature of these children which led them to death. Spring will bring release to the remaining three. They will leave the island then, and Rendal and Lem will find their parents, whose names Auntie has spoken.

"There is nothing to fear, child," says the goddess. "There will be splendour in winter that summer can never equal. In winter, the whole power and pride of nature is unloosed... Cold is the essence of the truth... In darkness, all thought is born... Dark is the single fabric from which we are all formed." This is a very different sort of darkness from the evil power in Susan Cooper's fantasy. It is akin to that dark night of the soul known to the mystics, from which they come into the light.

There is much of the quality of George MacDonald in this play. Its northernness, the character of the Goddess, the quality of goodness are all akin to him. It is a distillation of magic, a sequence in which time is suspended. Rendal and Lem willingly, Auntie unknowingly, accept a season of dream. They are assured of a happy awakening and believe the assurance.

In modern fantasy there is often a turning to old legends, legends sometimes retold in their own period and setting, or sometimes brought up to date. Events may be re-enacted that were once the stuff of ballad or folklore. Behind and deep within Catherine Storr's *Thursday*[103] lies one of the most magical of Border legends, that of Tam Lin who was taken by the Queen of Elfland and rescued by his faithful and valiant love, Janet. Catherine Storr has already written of friendship begun in dream and continued in reality in that moving and remarkable story, *Marianne Dreams*, in which a girl in bed with a long illness begins to draw pictures with a magic pencil. She brings a boy, also an invalid, into the world of her drawings to share the danger and fantastic adventure. In *Thursday*, a boy alone is in peril. The girl Bee is his protector, his rescuer. Thursday is an unwanted boy. His father is in prison; his step-mother is indifferent, even hostile. Bee, in contrast, has a good home and wise parents. She can give strength. Thursday disappears. He is last seen on a derelict bomb site near London. Old Mrs Smith at the general store apparently knows something: she is country-born, with an inherited knowledge of the Other People. "They've took him ... Them that's everywhere," she tells Bee. "I'm to blame. I should have known they were after him. The signs were there and I never read them."

157

Bee finds him after a long search, but it is only his living body which has been found. Far more difficult is the task of finding and releasing his true, inward self, taken captive by Them.

Tam Lin came riding with the fairy host on Hallowe'en, and Janet, awaiting him, caught and held him through every loathsome, enchanted form until he was himself again. Bee meets Thursday on the bombed site where he had disappeared. "They took me," he says. He knows, as Tam Lin knew, that he is in the power of an adversary and, like Tam Lin, he wants to come back. Only Bee can save him. He remembers strange lights, the trembling of the ground, a mound opening, music as of a flute and the sound of the feet of the Little People.

Bee holds him as Janet held Tam Lin. He struggles, and there is a bitter cry from those who know they have lost their victim. Music sounds and a voice cries out that Bee has conquered the unseen adversary. She finds Thursday safe in her arms, neither struggling nor inert, but holding firmly to her.

The Little People are not always hostile. They can be good friends and protective guides, as Jean and Donald happily discover in *Borrobil*[104], by the late William Croft Dickinson. They come to the wood at Beltane on May Day and see the Beltane fire lit. They meet Borrobil, a Scots cousin to Puck, and hear from him how that night the White King of Summer must fight and overcome the Black King of Winter. They are drawn into the far past and into an intricacy of adventures. They are always guarded by Borrobil, but they have a part to play: they must help a brave knight slay a dragon and win the Princess Finella. Jean experiences the greater danger, being nearly taken by malicious fairies, but Borrobil is at hand, and he brings both children safely home to witness the victory of the White King. In their own time and place again, they meet an old man of the village who dimly remembers having heard, in his boyhood, of Borrobil. Jean and Donald will not forget.

They meet Borrobil again in *The Eildon Tree*[105], where the magic is safer for them than it was long ago for Thomas the Rhymer when he met the Queen of Elfland by that tree. Finally, in *The Flag from the Isles*[106], they are present at Flodden and, after that lamentable battle, they see James the Fourth carried from the field, away north and over the sea to the western isles.

William Croft Dickinson was a scholar, an historian deeply learned in the history of early and medieval Scotland, whose scholarship was lit by imagination. The same combination of learning and creativeness is apparent in Lewis and Tolkien, and it is found again in Katharine Briggs, whose period of study is the seventeenth century and whose way into the past is equally illumined by learning and imagination. Her two tales of domestic magic, *Hobberdy Dick*[107] and *Kate Crackernuts*[108] (the latter a retelling of an old tale), are both superb stories, while her scholarly books, *The Anatomy of Puck* and *The Personnel of Fairyland*, are as entrancing as any legends.

Belief in the Good People was firmly held in the seventeenth century, throughout the Civil War and all its changes. Then, as Dr Briggs writes, "the authority of the past would have a sanctity which we could hardly conceive". But is there not, perhaps, nowadays a renewal of fantasy, of a sense of the mystery or even sanctity of the past, come from the trauma of the Second World War? We are closer now to the seventeenth century than we were seventy years ago.

We are returning to the past and its magic with the story-tellers as well as the scholars as our guides, and we are looking there for light. But in the seventeenth century fairy-lore was still part of the background of ordinary folk. Shakespeare and Milton knew this, and Milton, although he wrote more majestically of lost Eden, never wrote so entrancingly as when he told of Fairy Mab and of the homely and mischievous hobgoblins.

This is the world Katharine Briggs presents in *Hobberdy Dick*. Dick is the domestic fairy or hob of the Culvers who own a Manor in the Cotswolds. They are driven away during the Civil War and the Manor is bought by a wealthy Puritan merchant named Widdison, whom Dick dislikes intensely. Dick, however, still feels himself bound to the house, and he is curious about the new occupants. The family has some sympathetic members. There is the grandmother, Mrs Dimbleby, mother of Mr Widdison's first wife and grandmother to Joel, and there is Joel himself, only son of his father's first marriage, who has inherited his grandmother's gentleness. He is a born scholar, averse altogether from his merchant father's career. Dick is also fond of one of the younger children, Martha, but best of all he likes Anne, a poor gentlewoman employed to attend upon the somewhat vulgar and overbearing Mrs Widdison. Anne, it emerges later, is kin to the Culvers.

Anne remembers Hobberdy Dick, from her childhood, as "a little dark man with prick ears, dressed in clothes as ragged as cobwebs". Dick is known also to the cattleman, George Blatchford, a man of sound character who, cherishing the old ways, contrives to celebrate Christmas in the stable.

It is fortunate for the new family that their domestic hob and the Other People are still about and still, in a crisis, willing to be protective. The child Martha is stolen by a witch and hidden in an earth-barrow. Dick rallies all his own folk, including Old Grim from the ruined chapel in the churchyard. Anne, Joel and George come too. Only Anne can bring Martha out of captivity, by reading from the Bible and uttering the Holy Name. This the hobs, although not evil or malignant, do not care to hear. Dick shrinks from it and trembles. It is a power and mystery beyond any magic.

Martha is rescued but life does not return to normal because the Manor is haunted by a comic ghost, a miser who appears in the Widdisons' bedroom and keeps them awake by counting his money. He is got rid of, but a far worse haunting continues in the attic where once a child was murdered by his stepmother. Her guilty spirit has taken the form of the child. This horror is beyond Anne's power to remedy, good as she is. Only the grandmother, who has grown old in goodness, wisdom and faith, has the strength to exorcise this spirit.

"Come out," she calls, "and get to the place that is best for you, through the love of God." And so the spirit departs. Dick cowers in fear. The words pierce like fire, "almost consuming his being". The gentle old lady, having spent all her strength, dies in victory.

Apart (if it can be kept apart) from the magic, this tale is entrancingly full of country lore, and of humour and realism, and, like any good fairy-tale, it ends happily. Joel is allowed to go to Oxford, leaving his younger brother to follow their father in his business. Anne and he, in love from the first, are betrothed, and Anne proves to be an heiress. George and Martha find a silver cup bearing the united arms of her family and the Culvers, and Hobberdy Dick himself discovers some long lost family treasure. The Widdisons return to London, to the delight of Madam, and the Manor is left to Joel and Anne—and Hobberdy Dick. Anne, however, tells Joel that it is time to release him, for he is older even than the old family and he is longing to depart to his own place. She knows how to set him free. On the hearth Dick finds a little broom, some cream, a piece of bridal cake and two new suits, one green, one red. The cake and cream are proper offerings to a hearth-hob. To accept the broom would mean that he chooses to stay in service, whereas either of the suits would set him free. Wearing the green he would go into faery, but he chooses the red, which at once becomes part of him. It is the red of human blood. He suddenly feels the heat and weight of humanity and of age. Then his own good deeds for humankind through the centuries banish the heat and lift the weight and he goes forth singing. Anne and Joel see, for a moment, a glowing shape. He does not return, but the Manor remains a lucky and a happy place always.

The old tale retold by Dr Briggs, *Kate Crackernuts*, deals with the old theme of the wicked stepmother, but with a variation. In such tales there is usually an equally wicked step-sister but in *Kate Crackernuts* the step-sisters are devoted to each other and the stepmother is foiled by her own daughter.

In the original fairy-tale, the stepmother Queen casts a cruel spell upon the King's beautiful daughter: a witch in her service puts a sheep's head on the Princess. The step-sister, Kate Crackernuts, runs away with the poor girl. They come to the household of another king, whose son is compelled by magic to enter a fairy hill and dance himself into exhaustion. Kate follows and rescues him, as Janet saved Tam Lin.

Dr Briggs has expanded this plot into a novel, set in mid-seventeenth-century Galloway, just after the execution of Charles the First. The country is torn apart by the Civil War. Belief in witchcraft is very strong and there is a coven in the district. Instead of a King and Queen, we have Andrew Lindsay, a laird, his daughter Katherine and his second wife Grizel, with her daughter, Kate. The characters of the two girls are clearly defined. Katherine is gentle, though by no means weak; Kate is valiant, daring, lively and resourceful. The spell put upon Katherine is a psychological one, imposed by the witch Mallie Wood, who makes the poor girl *believe* that she wears an ugly sheep's head. Grizel tries to draw her own Kate into witchcraft, and takes her to a meeting of the coven of which she herself is head. The wild blood in Kate is stirred. She comes near yielding to the dreadful lure. But her love for Katherine is stronger, and she takes her away, across the Solway to England. They are followed by Grizel and Mallie Wood in another boat. A storm arises, and the two witches utter threats and curses. Katherine in pure innocence replies with a blessing, "God with you," and at the very speaking of the Holy Name the witches' boat goes a-whirling down and Grizel and Mallie Wood are drowned.

Over the border the two girls come to a squire's house where Kate finds shelter for Katherine, and where she herself works under the housekeeper. Like the prince in the old tale, the son of the house is spellbound and summoned away at full moon. Kate follows him, and, with the help of a small fairy who has taken a liking to her and whom she has rewarded with milk and meal, brings him back and, in the end, cures him of his bewitchment. Katherine, too, recovers and sees her own true bonny face.

There is a joyful homecoming and, soon afterwards, a double wedding. Kate is married to the young squire, Katherine to the tutor Gideon, a gentle scholar who has long loved her and whom she loves. The evil is all left behind (although Kate has her private agony for the death of her mother) and the tale ends with the bridal toast:

> May they live happy and die happy,
> And never drink out of a dry cappy.

Kate Crackernuts is a superb example of the re-enactment, the re-creation of a folk tale of old magic. This process of re-creation may well be continued, for the renaissance of wonder is, today, full of life and strength.

There are other worlds of myth or magic or dream in addition to the world of fairy-tale. Science fiction, also, has its marvels and its morals. So, too, have the half-magic woods and rivers and mountains which animals possess, with or without the occasional intrusion of man, and which are often happily and lovingly described. There is nothing to match the dream-loveliness, the pure poetry, of Walter de la Mare's *Three Royal Monkeys*, or, to give it its original and more alluring title, *The Three Mulla Mulgars*[109], but Richard Adams' *Watership Down*[110] has enchantment as well as natural realism and a profound sympathy with its animal characters. The characterisation here is strong, and, combined with the danger and excitement, it produces excellent drama. This long tale has, too, the old, undying allurement of the epic quest: the exile, the search for a new home, and eventual success.

Yet *Watership Down* has none of the evocativeness of *The Three Mulla Mulgars*, which is utterly fantastic and yet utterly real, another world, yet a world the poet makes credible and acceptable.

"On the borders of the Forest of Munza-Mulgar lived once an old grey fruit-monkey of the name of Mutt-matutta." She had three sons, the Royal Monkeys, and, as in all the best fairy-tales, the youngest, "who was a Nizza-Neela, Umanodda", Nod for short, is the hero. It is a long journey to Tishnar, "the wonderful, secret and quiet world beyond the Mulgars' lives". This is enchanted geography, a magic Odyssey, a coming at last to Paradise.

In lost Eden there was perfect companionship between man and beast and bird, between "all creatures great and small", newly made for His own delight by the Lord God. Man broke that unity, but there are many tales which seek to recover it, tales in which animals live a full life of mind and soul as well as body, tales in which there is comradeship again, in which all creatures go on a quest towards their own Paradise.

In addition to the realms of fairies, men and animals, there is the realm of the little folk who are not of faery: the dwarfs, who may be in touch with elfdom or be wholly of their own very earthy abode. *The Little Grey Men*[111] of B.B.'s narrative are of the latter sort. They are "the last gnomes in England", and anything less whimsical or "prettified" than their journey towards safety it would be impossible to find. In Hilda van Stockum's *King Oberon's Forest*[112] there are three dwarfs who like to keep themselves to themselves, but who are involved by Oberon both in the fairy and in the animal world when a fairy child is left on their doorstep. The events in the story could all be translated into an entirely human tale of a foundling baby, his effect on his reluctant guardians and their conversion to geniality. The little boy lost is sought by all the neighbours and eventually turns out to be a prince.

But the history of myth and magic, which could include so much of our literature, might meander like an endless river through meadows and woodland, past towns and in and out of caverns. Here it must stop, at least for a time.

There has been a century and more of domestic magic since the renaissance of wonder was ushered in by the Scots poet and

163

mystic and teller of tales. Has all that he brought us been continued? Today we need the Recovery, the Escape, the Consolation of fairy-tale more than ever. Perhaps all but one blessing and boon has been continued: is there today still *holiness* in the magic?

REFERENCES

If a U.S. edition of a work cited in text is currently available, that edition is listed here with full bibliographic information; otherwise a shortened reference to the original British or foreign edition is given.

1. Frances Browne, *Granny's Wonderful Chair* (London: Dent, 1963; reprint ed., 1975). Distributed by Biblio Distribution Center, Totowa, N.J.
2. George MacDonald, *Phantastes and Lilith* (Grand Rapids, Mich.: Eerdmans, 1964).
3. George MacDonald, *At the Back of the North Wind* (New York: Macmillan, 1964).
4. George MacDonald, *The Princess and the Goblin* (Bridgeport, Conn.: Airmont, 1967).
5. George MacDonald, *The Princess and Curdie* (Elgin, Ill.: Cook, 1979).
6. George MacDonald, *The Golden Key* (New York: Farrar, Straus & Giroux, 1976).
7. George MacDonald, *Ranald Bannerman's Boyhood* (Blackie, 1911).
8. Greville MacDonald, *George MacDonald and His Wife* (Allen and Unwin, 1924; reprint ed., New York: Johnson Reprint, n.d.).
9. Robert Lee Wolff, *The Golden Key* (Northford, Conn.: Elliot's Books, 1961).
10. George MacDonald, *Alec Forbes of Howglen* (New York: Garland, 1975).
11. John F. Campbell, *Popular Tales of the West Highlands*, 4 vols. (Detroit: Gale Research, 1969).
12. Robert Chambers, *Popular Rhymes of Scotland* (Detroit: Gale Research, 1969).
13. Erik Haugaard, trans., *The Complete Fairy Tales and Stories of Hans Andersen* (Gollancz, 1974).
14. Juliana Horatia Ewing, *Old-Fashioned Fairy Tales* (George Bell, n.d.).
15. Juliana Horatia Ewing, *The Land of Lost Toys*, from *Aunt Judy's Yearly*, vol. 6, ca. 1868.
16. Mary L. Molesworth, *The Cuckoo Clock* (1877; reprint ed., London: Dent, 1974). Distributed by Biblio Distribution Center, Totowa, N.J.
17. Mary L. Molesworth, *The Tapestry Room* (New York: Garland, 1976).
18. Mary L. Molesworth, *The Children of the Castle* (New York: Garland, 1976).
19. Mary L. Molesworth, *Four Winds Farm* (1887; reprint ed., New York: Garland, 1976).
20. Mary de Morgan, *The Necklace of Princess Fiorimonde and Other Stories* (New York: Garland, 1977).
21. E. Nesbit, *Five Children and It* (Elmsford, N.Y.: British Book Center, 1974).
22. E. Nesbit, *The Phoenix and the Carpet* (Elmsford, N.Y.: British Book Center, 1974).
23. E. Nesbit, *Story of the Amulet* (Elmsford, N.Y.: British Book Center, 1974).
24. E. Nesbit, *House of Arden* (New York: Dutton, 1968).
25. E. Nesbit, *Harding's Luck* (Elmsford, N.Y.: British Book Center, 1974).
26. E. Nesbit, *The Enchanted Castle* (Elmsford, N.Y.: British Book Center, 1974).

27. E. Nesbit, *The Magic City* (Benn, 1930).
28. E. Nesbit, *Wet Magic* (Fisher Unwin, 1926).
29. E. Nesbit, *Wonderful Garden* (Elmsford, N.Y.: British Book Center, 1974).
30. Doris Langley Moore, *E. Nesbit* (Benn, 1967).
31. Rudyard Kipling, *Puck of Pook's Hill* (Macmillan, 1926).
32. Rudyard Kipling, *Rewards and Fairies* (Macmillan, 1930).
33. John Masefield, *The Midnight Folk* (Heinemann, 1927).
34. John Masefield, *The Box of Delights* (Heinemann, 1935).
35. Walter de la Mare, *Poems, 1901-1918* (Constable, 1928).
36. Walter de la Mare, *Stuff and Nonsense* (Constable, 1927).
37. Walter de la Mare, "Miss Jemima," from *Broomsticks* (Constable, 1925).
38. Walter de la Mare, *The Lord Fish* (Faber, 1939).
39. Walter de la Mare, *Crossings* (Collins, 1923).
40. Walter de la Mare, comp., *Come Hither* (New York: Knopf, 1957).
41. James Stephens, *Deidre* (New York: Macmillan, 1970).
42. James Stephens, *The Land of Youth* (Macmillan, 1924).
43. James Stephens, *Crock of Gold* (New York: Macmillan, 1960).
44. Patricia Lynch, *A Storyteller's Childhood* (Dent, 1947).
45. Patricia Lynch, *The Turf-Cutter's Donkey* (Dent, 1934).
46. Patricia Lynch, *The Turf-Cutter's Donkey Goes Visiting* (Dent, 1935).
47. Patricia Lynch, *Brogeen Follows the Magic Tune* (New York: Macmillan, 1968).
48. Patricia Lynch, *Guests at the Beech Tree* (Burke, 1964).
49. C. S. Lewis, *The Lion, the Witch and the Wardrobe* (New York: Macmillan, 1970).
50. C. S. Lewis, *Of Other Worlds: Essays and Stories* (New York: Harcourt Brace Jovanovich, 1975).
51. C. S. Lewis, *Surprised by Joy: The Shape of My Early Life* (New York: Harcourt Brace Jovanovich, 1966).
52. C. S. Lewis, *Perelandra* (New York: Macmillan, 1968).
53. C. S. Lewis, *Prince Caspian* (New York: Macmillan, 1970).
54. C. S. Lewis, *Voyage of the Dawn Treader* (New York: Macmillan, 1970).
55. C. S. Lewis, *The Silver Chair* (New York: Macmillan, 1970).
56. C. S. Lewis, *The Horse and His Boy* (New York: Macmillan, 1970).
57. C. S. Lewis, *The Magician's Nephew* (New York: Macmillan, 1970).
58. C. S. Lewis, *The Last Battle* (New York: Macmillan, 1970).
59. J. R. R. Tolkien, *Tree and Leaf* (Boston: Houghton Mifflin, 1965).
60. Hilda Ellis Davidson, *Gods and Myths of Northern Europe* (Penguin, 1969).
61. J. R. R. Tolkien, *The Hobbit* (Boston: Houghton Mifflin, 1938).
62. J. R. R. Tolkien, *The Fellowship of the Ring* (Boston: Houghton Mifflin, 1967).
63. J. R. R. Tolkien, *The Two Towers* (Boston, Houghton Mifflin, 1976).
64. J. R. R. Tolkien, *The Return of the King* (Boston: Houghton Mifflin, 1967).
65. Alison Uttley, *A Traveller in Time* (Faber, 1939).
66. Meta Mayne Reid, *Sandy and the Hollow Book* (Faber, 1961).
67. Meta Mayne Reid, *With Angus in the Forest* (Faber, 1963).
68. Lucy M. Boston, *The Children of Green Knowe* (New York: Harcourt Brace Jovanovich, 1977).
69. Lucy Boston, *The Chimneys of Green Knowe* (Faber, 1961).
70. Lucy M. Boston, *An Enemy at Greene Knowe* (New York: Harcourt Brace Jovanovich, 1979).
71. Penelope Lively, *The Driftway* (Heinemann, 1974).
72. William Mayne, *A Game of Dark* (New York: Dutton, 1971).

73. William Mayne, *Earthfasts* (New York: Dutton, 1966).
74. Ray Bradbury, *The Halloween Tree* (New York: Bantam Books, 1974).
75. T. H. White, *The Sword in the Stone* (New York: Putnam, 1939).
76. T. H. White, *The Witch in the Wood* (Collins, 1940).
77. T. H. White, *The Ill-made Knight* (Collins, 1941).
78. Mary Stewart, *The Crystal Cave* (New York: Fawcett, 1979).
79. Mary Stewart, *The Hollow Hills* (New York: Fawcett, 1979).
80. Alan Garner, *The Weirdstone of Brisingamen* (New York: William Collins, 1979).
81. Alan Garner, *The Moon of Gomrath* (New York: William Collins, 1979).
82. Alan Garner, *The Owl Service* (Collins, 1967).
83. Alan Garner, *Elidor* (New York: William Collins, 1979).
84. Susan Cooper, *Over Sea, Under Stone* (New York: Harcourt Brace Jovanovich, 1979).
85. Susan Cooper, *The Dark Is Rising* (New York: Atheneum, 1976).
86. Susan Cooper, *Greenwitch* (New York: Atheneum, 1977).
87. Winifred Finlay, *The Singing Stones* (Harrap, 1970).
88. Winifred Finlay, *Beadbonny Ash* (Harrap, 1973).
89. Rosemary Harris, *The Seal-Singing* (New York: Macmillan, 1974).
90. Ronald Lockley, *The Seal Woman* (New York: Avon, 1977).
91. George Mackay Brown, *The Two Fiddlers* (Chatto & Windus, 1974).
92. Ursula K. LeGuin, *The Wizard of Earthsea* (New York: Bantam Books, 1975).
93. Ursula K. LeGuin, *The Tombs of Atuan* (New York: Bantam Books, 1975).
94. Ursula K. LeGuin, *The Farthest Shore* (New York: Bantam Books, 1975).
95. William Ready, *Understanding Tolkien and The Lord of the Rings* (New York: Warner Books, 1969).
96. Philippa Pearce, *Tom's Midnight Garden* (New York: Dell, 1979).
97. Helen Cresswell, *Up the Pier* (New York: Macmillan, 1972).
98. Joy Chant, *Red Moon and Black Mountain* (New York: Dutton, 1976).
99. Joan Aiken, *Winterthing* (New York: Harcourt Brace Jovanovich, 1972).
100. Joan Aiken, *The Wolves of Willoughby Chase* (New York: Dell, 1968).
101. Joan Aiken, *Black Hearts in Battersea* (New York: Dell, 1969).
102. Joan Aiken, *Whispering Mountain* (New York: Dell, 1971).
103. Catherine Storr, *Thursday* (New York: Harper & Row, 1972).
104. William Croft Dickinson, *Borrobil* (Cape, Puffin, 1967).
105. William Croft Dickinson, *The Eildon Tree* (Cape, 1944).
106. William Croft Dickinson, *The Flag from the Isles* (Cape, 1951).
107. Katharine M. Briggs, *Hobberdy Dick* (New York: Greenwillow, 1977).
108. Katharine Briggs, *Kate Crackernuts* (Alden Press, 1965).
109. Walter de la Mare, *The Three Mulla Mulgars* (Duckworth, 1921).
110. Richard Adams, *Watership Down* (New York:Macmillan, 1975).
111. B. B., *The Little Grey Men* (Eyre & Spottiswoode, Puffin, 1962).
112. Hilda von Stockum, *King Oberon's Forest* (Constable, 1958).

INDEX

Stephens, James, 77-8
Stewart, Mary, 133
Stockum, Hilda von, 163
Storr, Catherine, 157-8
Sutcliff, Rosemary, 126

Tolkien, J. R. R., 5, 9, 84, 86, 88, 101-125, 151-2;
    Beowulf and the Critics, 107;

The Hobbit, 9, 112-15; *Lord of the Rings*, 6, 115-25; *Tree and Leaf*, 101

Uttley, Alison, 126-7

White, T. H., 133
Williams, Charles, 86
Wolff, Robert Lee, 11

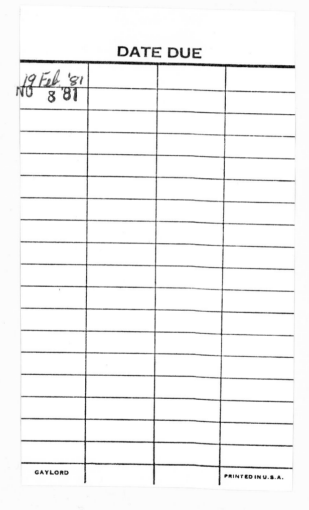

DATE DUE